THE COMPLETE

Z GRILLS

WOOD PELLET GRILL AND SMOKER

COOKBOOK

TASTY AND DELICIOUS RECIPES TO SMOKE, MEAT, BAKE OR ROAST LIKE A CHEF

CAROL SLAYTON

CONTENTS

INTRODUCTION..**7**

What IS Z Grills Wood Pellet Grill? 7

How does Z Grills Wood Pellet Grill work? 7

Why People Choose the Z Grills Wood Pellet Grill? 7

How to Use the Z Grills Wood Pellet Grill? 9

How to Clean and Care for Your Z Grills Wood Pellet Grill? 11

BAKING RECIPES..**13**

Cheese Mac 13

Chocolate Almond Cake 14

Butternut Squash Macaroni And Cheese 15

Cake With Smoked Berry Sauce 16

Vanilla Chocolate Chip Cookies 17

Savory Beaver Tails..18

Grilled Bourbon Pecan Pie 19

Cast Iron Pineapple Upside Down Cake 20

Mint Butter Chocolate Chip Cookies 21

Baked Irish Creme Cake 22

Irish Soda Bread 23

S'mores Dip Skillet 24

SEAFOOD RECIPES **25**

Seared Ahi Tuna Steak With Soy Sauce 25

Dijon-smoked Halibut 26

Barbecued Shrimp 27

Grilled Garlic Shrimp With Cajun Dip 28

Bacon Wrapped Scallops 29

Hot-smoked Salmon 30

Thai-style Swordfish Steaks With Peanut Sauce 31

Honey-soy Garlic Salmon 32

Grilled Trout With Citrus & Basil 33

Cold-smoked Salmon Gravlax...34

Grilled Fresh Fish 35

Grilled Lemon Lobster Tails 36

Grilled Garlic Lobster Tails 37

PORK RECIPES **38**

Bbq Pork Shoulder Steaks 38

Pork Belly Burnt Ends 39

Bangers And Potato Mash 40

Baked Maple And Brown Sugar Bacon 41

Sweet Bacon 42

Grilled German Sausage With A Smoky Traeger Twist 43

Pork Tenderloin With Bourbon Peaches 44

Smoked Pork Tomato Tamales 45

Grilled Sweet Pork Tenderloin 46

Smoked Ham 47

Mini Sausage Rolls 48

Beer Braised Pork Belly And Beef 49

Grilled Prosciutto Wrapped Asparagus 50

VEGETABLES RECIPES **51**

Roasted Jalapeno Cheddar Deviled Eggs 51

Red Potato Grilled Lollipops 52

Grilled Asparagus & Honey-glazed Carrots 53

Blt Pasta Salad 54

Roasted Green Beans With Bacon 55

Grilled Zucchini Squash Spears 56

Roasted Artichokes With Garlic Butter 57

Grilled Asparagus And Hollandaise Sauce 58

Baked Winter Squash Au Gratin 59

Baked Breakfast Mini Quiches 60

Roasted Sweet Potato Steak Fries 61

Mashed Red Potatoes 62

Roasted New Potatoes 63

POULTRY RECIPES **64**

Delicious Smoked Turketta 64

Smoked Ditch Chicken 65

Grilled Honey Chicken Kabobs 66

Nashville Spiced Smoked Chicken 67

Spiced Cornish Hens With Cilantro Chutney 68

Lemon Chicken Breast 69

Savory Jerk Chicken Wings 70

Smoked Thanksgiving Turkey 71

Grilled Whole Chicken Stuffed Sausage And Apple 72

Easy Bbq Chicken Wings 73

Asian Chicken Sliders 74

Lollipop Drumsticks 75

Lemon Cajun Chicken Carbonara 76

APPETIZERS AND SNACKS **77**

Bayou Wings With Cajun Rémoulade 77

Chuckwagon Beef Jerky 78

Simple Cream Cheese Sausage Balls 79

Pigs In A Blanket 80

Sriracha & Maple Cashews 81

Smoked Turkey Sandwich 82

Pulled Pork Loaded Nachos 83

Jalapeño Poppers With Chipotle Sour Cream 84

Grilled Guacamole 85

Bacon Pork Pinwheels (kansas Lollipops) 86

Citrus-infused Marinated Olives 87

Roasted Red Pepper Dip 88

Deviled Eggs With Smoked Paprika 89

BEEF LAMB AND GAME RECIPES **90**

Reverse Sear Tomahawk Chop 90

Cheddar Bacon Beef Burgers 91

Grilled Rib Eyes With Hasselback Sweet Potatoes 92

Slow Smoked Spiced Beef 93

Salt & Pepper Beer-braised Beef Ribs 94

Easy Breakfast Cheeseburger 95

Flavour Tri Tip Burnt Ends 96

Garlic Parmesan Grilled Filet Mignon 97

Bbq Brisket Breakfast Tacos 98

Roasted Prime Rib With Mustard And Herbs De Provence 99

Bacon-wrapped Elk Steaks 100

Ancho Pepper Rubbed Brisket 101

Smoked New York Steaks 102

COCKTAILS RECIPES **103**

Smoked Pumpkin Spice Latte 103

Grilled Peach Mint Julep 104

Smoked Pineapple Hotel Nacional Cocktail 105

Sunset Margarita 106

Smoked Pomegranate Lemonade Cocktail 107

Smoke And Bubz Cocktail 108

Smoky Scotch & Ginger Cocktail 109

Smoked Apple Cider 110

Bacon Old-fashioned Cocktail 111

Smoked Cold Brew Coffee 112

INTRODUCTION

What IS Z Grills Wood Pellet Grill?

Wood Pellet grills utilize ignited wood pellets and a system of fans to heat food to a specific temperature, quite like an outdoor convection oven. Pellet grills can be used to smoke, grill, bake and even braise food. Nearly anything you make in a standard oven can be made on a pellet grill.

How does Z Grills Wood Pellet Grill work?

The heat is generated from wood pellets that are placed in a chamber called a "pellet hopper." Those pellets move through an auger to a fire pot, which heats the entire cooking chamber of the grill. Through a fan system, heat and smoke are dispensed throughout the grill, providing a naturally rich and woody flavor from the pellets. Though pellet grills certainly share some characteristics of your traditional grills, there are a couple of major differences that set pellet grills apart: most notably, the combination of deep flavor, versatility and efficiency.

Why People Choose the Z Grills Wood Pellet Grill?

1.Z Grills WOOD PELLET GRILL IS EASY TO USE

One of the greatest features of a pellet grill is the fact they're easy to use. Simply fill the hopper with food-grade wood pellets, empty the ash pail, and select your desired temperature and smoke level. The pellet grill takes over from there as an electric auger feeds the burn pot with wood pellets from the hopper.

Once you set the temperature, the pellet grill maintains it and feeds wood pellets as needed. Pellet grills are highly precise with temperature control from their lowest to highest settings (180-500 degrees on many grills).

For even more accurate control, grill blankets are available to help pellet grills hold in more heat and smoke. They maintain even more consistent temperatures throughout the entire year, but they're especially useful in the winter months when outside temperatures drop.

Pellet grills are also easy to clean when you're finished cooking. Whether it's a quick clean-up or a deeper clean, no effort takes longer than 15 minutes to maintain your grill.

2. SET IT & FORGET IT

With pellet grills, you can set it and walk away. Since the grill does all the work, you get a wood-fired taste without having to constantly feed logs or wood chunks. Overall, pellet grills do not require as much time or attention, and there's no need to constantly check the grill temperature or level of smoke.

Newer models even monitor temperature levels from the palm of your hand. Traeger and Camp Chef now both feature, easy-to-use, WiFi controlling technology. Change the temperature, adjust smoke levels, and receive notifications from your phone.

3. VERSATILITY TO COOK ANYTHING

Naturally, a pellet grill is great for smoking and grilling, but it's also the centerpiece for much more. All of your favorite dishes that are usually cooked inside can now be done outdoors. Think of it as a kitchen in your backyard where you can perfectly cook anything with confidence.

➢ BBQ

Traditional smokers have set the BBQ bar for a long time and are debated to provide a better smoke. On the opposite side of that argument are pellet grills. Pellet grills are now recognized for their quality and are even sanctioned in contests sponsored by the Kansas City Barbeque Society (KCBS), winning many bbq competitions in recent years.

The combination of smoke quality and convenience with pellet grills is unbeatable. Taste all of your barbecue favorites from the comfort of your own backyard. Pick your favorite wood pellet flavors, set the grill on low and go. You'll love the beautiful smoke ring, tenderness, and delicious flavor you get from home cooked ribs, pulled pork, beef brisket, chicken quarters and wings. Fresh salmon, trout, and even sides such as mac and cheese are wonderfully smoky and tasty.

➢ BAKE

Anything cooked in an oven can be done in a pellet grill. Pellet grills primarily work as a convection oven. Indirect heat and smoke are produced from the burn pot and blown around the pellet grill for a perfect, evenly cooked finish. Bake breads, cakes, pies, breakfast casseroles, and delicious, wood-fired pizzas. Plus, when you bake your favorites outside in the summer months, you avoid heating up your house and kitchen.

> **GRILL**

For many of our common grilling favorites–such as summer burgers and hot dogs–there's a time when we need to turn up the heat. Pork chops and your favorite cuts of steak or chicken are fabulous when cooked over a wood fire. Don't forget your vegetables too!

Pellet grills used to only have an indirect heat option, but that has changed in recent years. To improve the grilling feature, many manufacturers now offer models with perforated drip trays, direct heat over the burn pot, and/or temperatures up to 500°. This allows your burgers and steaks to sizzle and get those beautiful grill marks and a good crust on the outside, while still preserving a medium to rare center.

4. GREAT WOOD-FIRED FLAVORS

While there are many grilling options out there, nothing produces better tasting food than a pellet grill. Fuel flavors your food and with wood-fired flavors are superior to gas and charcoal alternatives. All of your favorite dishes are simply better on a pellet grill.

With pellet grills, you also have flavor options when choosing wood pellets for your grill. Each pellet flavor, or type of wood, has a unique taste that naturally complements and enhances your favorite foods. Specific hardwood blends are also available. Experiment with different food-grade wood pellet options and find the flavors you and your family enjoy the most.

How to Use the Z Grills Wood Pellet Grill?

For wood pellet newcomers, pellet grills and smokers are an excellent way to get into barbecue. Learn how to get the best out of your wood cooker with our step-by-step guide to using a pellet smoker grill.

1. Season your pellet smoker.

Before we do anything, we need to season the smoker. This is a crucial step for any type of new smoker, and helps protect it from the negative effects of long term continuous use. The basic premise is to apply cooking oil to the grates and inside of the chamber and then take the smoker on a 'dry run' without food. This will cook the oil onto the inside surfaces of the smoker, forming a protective layer across it.

After you have seasoned it, leave the smoker to cool and rest for at least 24 hours before using properly.

2. Preheat your smoker.

A big pain with charcoal grills is heating them up. Lighting them and keeping them at a good temperature can be tricky. Not so with a pellet grill. They work much in the same way as an oven.

With your grill plugged in to an electric outlet or socket, switch it on and select your target temperature. If you're going for barbecue smoking, choose 225°F (107°C).

Most smokers will take about 10 minutes to preheat and come to temperature.

You should hear a dull roar come from the smoker as it heats up. This is the motorized auger and firebox springing into action, and is a good sign that your smoker is working and warming up.

Pro tip: While pellet smokers do have a temperature gauge on their control display, it's not unusual for these to be inaccurate by up to about 20°F either way. Get a dual probe smoker thermometer. These allow you to simultaneously measure cooking and internal meat temperatures. The best models are more accurate than the majority of built-in gauges.

3. Add your meat.

With your pellet smoker now running at target temperature, carefully place your meat on the smoker grates. For the best results, place the food in the middle of the grate. This will ensure that the meat is far away enough from the heat to not dry out, but close enough to be cooked at temperature.

4. Pay attention to fat content.

A mistake that a lot of BBQ newcomers make is with the meat itself. Meat that is too lean can dry out quickly, whereas meat with too much fat content can get in the way of the smoke working its way into the flesh of the meat.

If you choose to smoke a cut like brisket, then be sure that you trim the layer of fat on it to about ½ inch thick before putting it on the smoker.

How to Clean and Care for Your Z Grills Wood Pellet Grill?

➢ BETWEEN EACH COOK

For quick cleanup between cookouts, you don't need to do anything too dramatic. In fact, our patented Ash Cleanout system makes it as simple as pulling a knob. Before you fire up the grill each time, just empty the ash into the cup, and you're good to go. It's almost too easy.

Don't forget about the internal temperature probe. You'll want to clean it between each cook. It's located on the right side of the cooking chamber and is about the size of a pencil. Our goal is to keep it looking silver. To do this mixt a vinegar/water solution and use a scouring pad. Often times if your temperature does not read accurately it's because too much smoke has been build up.

Besides emptying the burn cup, you may want to spot clean between cook sessions as well. This can be as simple as wiping away grease spots or food residue on the lid or side shelf. You should also scrape down the grill grates with a wire grill brush or spatula before you start cooking to avoid a burnt taste on your food.

If you take these small steps toward keeping your pellet grill clean, any deeper cleaning you do will be much easier.

➢ EXTERIOR

Safety first! Make sure your grill is totally cool, then unplug it from its power source.

Empty the pellet hopper to prevent your pellets from getting wet or coming into contact with cleaning substances.

Spray stainless steel cleaner on the painted or stainless steel surfaces of your grill. Avoid spraying any plastic components. (You can also use hot, soapy water-it just may not work as quickly!)

Let the cleaner sit for about 30 seconds to give it a chance to break down grease and smoke stains.

Wipe off the cleaner with a clean paper towel or rag. Wipe with the grain if you're cleaning stainless steel or in circles, if you're cleaning a painted surface.

Repeat the process once more to clean off any remaining grease or smoke. With a rag, rinse thoroughly if you used soapy water.

Allow to dry for at least 24 hours before cooking, and double-check that the hopper has no water in it before reloading pellets.

➢ **INTERIOR**

Pull the Ash Cleanout knob and empty the ash from the burn cup.

Open the lid and remove the cooking grate, any extra racks, drip tray, and heat diffuser plate from inside the grill. Pay attention to how these pieces are installed (or even take a picture) so you'll have an easier time reassembling your grill.

Use a wet/dry vacuum with a hose attachment to remove loose ash and debris.

Look for places inside your grill where grease has built up. Use something with a flat edge (a paint stick, pan scraper, etc.) to dislodge and remove it.

Use hot, soapy water and a rag you aren't attached to wash the interior of your grill, as well as each piece you pulled out.

Repeat the process until most of the grease buildup is gone.

With a rag, rinse thoroughly if you used soapy water and allow everything to dry.

Cover the heat diffuser plate and drip tray with aluminum foil for easier cleaning next time (you can simply throw away and replace the foil rather than scrubbing off the grease).

Allow to dry for at least 24 hours before cooking, and double-check that the hopper has no water in it before reloading pellets.

BAKING RECIPES

Cheese Mac

| Servings: 6 - 10 | Cooking Time: 60 Minutes |

Ingredients:

- 5 Tbsp All-Purpose Flour
- 4 Strips Bacon
- Black Pepper
- 2 Cups Breadcrumbs
- 4 Oz Brie
- 4 Oz Brie Cheese
- ½ Cup Butter, Melted
- 12 Oz Cheddar Cheese, Grated
- 3 Cloves Garlic, Minced
- 2 Tbsp Extra Virgin Olive Oil
- 1 Tsp Fresh Grated Nutmeg
- 1 Tsp Ground Cayenne
- 8 Oz, Grated Gruyere Cheese
- 1 Cup Heavy Cream
- 1, Minced Jalapeno Pepper
- 4 Oz Mozzarella Cheese, Grated
- 2 Tbsp Parsley, Minced Fresh
- 12 Oz Raclette
- To Taste Salt
- 5 Tbsp Unsalted Butter
- 4 Oz Whole Milk, Warm
- 1 Yellow Onion, Diced

Directions:

1. Supply your smoker with wood pellets and follow the start-up procedure. Preheat the grill, with the lid closed, to 350° F. Bring a large saucepan of water to a boil. Add the pasta and cook according to the package instructions for al dente. Drain.

2. Heat the oil in a large saucepan over medium-high heat.

3. Add the onion and cook for about 5 minutes, stirring often, until lightly colored, then add the garlic and the jalapeño and cook for 2 more minutes.

4. Reduce the heat to medium, add the butter, and stir until melted. Add the flour and cook, stirring often, for 5 minutes to form a light roux.

5. Add the cheeses, the milk, and cream, reduce the heat to medium-low, and cook, stirring often, until the cheese is melted, and a smooth sauce comes together, about 7 minutes.

6. Stir in the cayenne and truffle oil, then add the pasta and stir to fully coat it in the sauce. Season with salt and pepper. Transfer the mixture to a 12-inch cast-iron skillet and cover with aluminum foil.

7. Place on the grill and bake for 20 minutes. Remove the foil and cover the mac and cheese with the breadcrumbs.

8. Return to the grill and bake for another 15 to 20 minutes, until the cheese is bubbling and the breadcrumbs are golden brown. Serve family style right out of the skillet.

Chocolate Almond Cake

Servings: 8

Cooking Time: 50 Minutes

Ingredients:

- 7 oz good quality dark chocolate; melted
- 5 eggs; separated
- Pinch salt
- 6.5 oz caster sugar
- 7 oz butter; cubed at room temperature
- 7 oz ground almonds
- 1 oz cocoa powder
- 1 tsp. baking powder
- Icing sugar; for dusting

Directions:

1. Supply your smoker with wood pellets and follow the start-up procedure. Preheat the grill, with the lid closed, to 347 °F.

2. Beat together the butter and sugar until light and fluffy. Then beat in the yolks, one at a time.

3. Gently fold in the almonds.

4. Add the melted chocolate and mix well.

5. Beat the egg whites with a pinch of salt in a separate bowl until stiff.

6. Sift the baking powder and cocoa powder into the cake mix and fold in gently, then fold in the egg whites.

7. Pour the mix into an 8.5" round spring form cake tin (greased and lined), smooth over, and bake in the center of the grill for about 50 minutes. If the top starts to dry out after 25-30 minutes, cover with foil.

Butternut Squash Macaroni And Cheese

Servings: 2

Cooking Time: 50 Minutes

Ingredients:

- 1 Medium butternut squash
- 2 Cup macaroni, uncooked
- 1 Small yellow onion
- 1/2 Cup chicken broth
- 1 Cup milk
- salt
- pepper
- 1 Cup cheese, grated

Directions:

1. Supply your smoker with wood pellets and follow the start-up procedure. Preheat the grill, with the lid closed, to 225° F.

2. Puncture butternut squash with a fork several times and place on grill grate. Cook until tender, about 40 minutes to an hour. When cooked, scoop out meat and discard seeds. Grill: 225 °F

3. Cook elbow macaroni according to package instructions. Drain and set aside.

4. In a medium skillet, sauté chopped onion until fragrant and golden. Add broth, milk, salt, onions and butternut squash to a food processor. Puree until smooth and creamy. Add salt and pepper to taste.

5. Pour pureed sauce over cooked noodles and add the shredded cheese. Stir to melt the cheese and add milk to reach desired consistency. Serve warm. Enjoy!

Cake With Smoked Berry Sauce

<table>
<tr><td>Servings: 12</td><td>Cooking Time: 90 Minutes</td></tr>
</table>

Ingredients:

- 12 Oz Blackberries
- 18 Oz Blueberries, Fresh
- 1/4 Cup Brown Sugar
- 2 Tsp Cinnamon, Ground
- 4 Eggs
- 2 Tbsp Flour
- 1 3/4 Cup Granulated Sugar
- 1 Lemon, Juice & Zest
- 1/2 Cup Unsalted Butter
- 3.4 Ounce Box Vanilla Instant Pudding Mix
- 3/4 Cup Vegetable Oil
- 3/4 Cup Water
- 1 Cup White Wine
- 1 Box Yellow Cake Mix

Directions:

1. Fire up your Grill and set to Smoke mode. If using a gas or charcoal grill, set it up for low, indirect heat. Supply your smoker with wood pellets and follow the start-up procedure. Preheat the grill, with the lid closed, to 450° F.

2. Place blueberries and blackberries on a sheet tray, then transfer to upper shelf of smoking cabinet. Make sure that the sear slide and side dampers are open, then preheat the grill, with the lid closed, to 375° F, to ensure the cabinet maintains temperature between 225° F and 250° F. Smoke for 30 to 45 minutes.

3. Place cast iron skillet on grill grate. Add sugar, lemon juice and zest, and wine to skillet. Stir with a wooden spoon until sugar dissolves, then add berries from smoking cabinet.

4. Simmer berries for 15 minutes, then remove sauce from grill to cool.

5. While berries are smoking, prepare cake pans and batter. Grease and flour 2 - 9-inch round cake pans. Set aside.

6. In a large mixing bowl, combine cake mix, brown sugar, granulated sugar, pudding mix, cinnamon, eggs, water, oil, and white wine. Using a hand mixer, mix on low speed for 1 minute, then slowly increase mixing speed to high, and beat an additional 2 to 3 minutes, or until batter is smooth.

7. Evenly distribute batter among cake pans, then place pans on grill shelf and bake at 350° F, for 25 to 30 minutes, or until a toothpick inserted comes out clean. Remove from grill and set aside to cool slightly.

8. While cake is cooling, prepare glaze. Melt butter with sugar in a sauce pot on the grill. Stir for 3 minutes, then add wine. Remove from grill and set aside.

9. Turn out cake onto a sheet tray lined with parchment. Use a toothpick to poke holes in the cake, then slowly pour hot glaze over cake.

10. Spread half of smoked berry sauce on top of one layer, then place second cake layer on top. Pour additional sauce on top of cake and dust with powdered sugar, if desired. Serve warm, or room temperature.

Vanilla Chocolate Chip Cookies

Servings: 12   Cooking Time: 20 Minutes

Ingredients:

- 3/4 cup brown sugar
- 3/4 cup white sugar
- 1 stick butter, room temp
- 2 eggs
- 1 tsp vanilla

- 2 1/2 cups flour
- 1/2 tsp salt
- 1 tsp baking soda
- 1 cup Chocolate Chips

Directions:

1. Cream your butter and sugar together in a mixing bowl using a hand mixer or stand mixer on medium speed for about 4-5 minutes.
2. Once the butter is creamed, add the eggs and vanilla. Continue mixing for an additional minute.
3. Put flour, salt, and baking soda in a sifter. Sift it into your creamed butter mixture.
4. Scrape the sides of your mixing bowl with a rubber spatula, and then turn your mixer on to low speed.
5. Let it mix a little, and then scrape the sides again. Stop mixing when there are one or two streaks of flour left in the cookie dough.
6. Scrape the sides of your bowl and pour in a cup of chocolate chips, and turn the mixer to low again to mix the chocolate. It should take just a few turns for the chocolate pieces to be well incorporated.
7. Line a large baking sheet with parchment paper. Using a medium cookie scoop (about 1.5 tbsp), drop evenly spaced dollops of cookie dough onto the cookie sheet.
8. Supply your smoker with wood pellets and follow the start-up procedure. Preheat the grill, with the lid closed, to 350° F. Place the cookie sheet in your smoker, and let them cook for about 12 minutes.
9. Let them sit on a cooling rack while you continue to cook the additional cookies.
10. Cool for a few minutes to let cookies set.
11. Enjoy!

Savory Beaver Tails

Servings: 8

Cooking Time: 2 Minutes

Ingredients:

- 2 Tbsp Butter, Melted
- 1 Tbsp Cinnamon, Ground
- 1 Egg
- 2 1/2 Cups Flour, All-Purpose
- 1/2 Cup Milk, Warm
- 1/2 Tsp Salt
- 1 Tsp Sugar
- 1/2 Tsp Vanilla
- 1 L Vegetable Oil
- 1/4 Cup Water, Warm
- 2 1/2 Tsp Active Yeast, Instant

Directions:

1. In a small bowl, combine water, milk, yeast, and sugar. Let it sit for about 10 minutes or until frothy.

2. In another bowl, pour in the flour and make a well in the middle. Pour in butter, sugar, salt, vanilla and egg. Mix everything together until the dough is smooth. Knead for about 5 minutes and set the dough in a greased bowl. Cover with a towel and set aside for about an hour, or until the dough has doubled in size.

3. After one hour, supply your smoker with wood pellets and follow the start-up procedure. Preheat the grill, with the lid open, to 450° F.Pour 1L of vegetable oil into a cast iron pan and place on the grates of your Grill. Keep your flame broiler closed so as to prevent grease flareups. Preheat the oil so that it is 350 degrees F.

4. While you"re waiting for the oil to heat up, punch down the dough and separate into 8 small balls. Shape each piece of dough into a flat circle. Fry the dough in the preheated oil for about 1 minute per side, or until the dough is golden brown.

5. Sprinkle with cinnamon sugar immediately, or top with your desired toppings. Enjoy!

Grilled Bourbon Pecan Pie

Servings: 6

Cooking Time: 45 Minutes

Ingredients:

- 2 Tbsp Bourbon
- 1/2 Cup Brown Sugar
- 1/3 Cup Unsalted Butter, Melted
- 1/2 Cup Light, 1/2 Cup Dark Corn Syrup
- 3 Egg
- 1/4 Tsp Hickory Honey Smoked Salt
- Decoration Pecan
- 1 1/4 Cup Chopped Pecans, Coarsely Broken
- 1 Prepared Or Homemade Pie Shell, Deep
- 1/2 Cup Sugar
- 1 Tsp Vanilla Extract

Directions:

1. Supply your smoker with wood pellets and follow the start-up procedure. Preheat the grill, with the lid closed, to 375° F. Meanwhile, prepare your pie crust in a 9 cast iron skillet or heat proof pie plate.

2. In a large bowl, beat the eggs until smooth. Add the brown sugar and white sugar and mix until smooth. Add the light corn syrup, dark corn syrup, vanilla, bourbon, melted butter, and Hickory Honey Salt. Mix until smooth. Stir in your chopped pecans and pour into the pie crust. Top with the whole pecans, if desired.

3. Grill covered for 35-45 minutes, until the pie is just set around the edges but still has a slight jiggle in the center.

4. Allow the pie to cool completely before slicing. Enjoy!

Cast Iron Pineapple Upside Down Cake

Servings: 6

Cooking Time: 40 Minutes

Ingredients:

- 1/4 Cup butter, melted
- 1 Cup brown sugar
- 20 Ounce Pineapple, sliced
- 6 Ounce maraschino cherries
- 1 Whole Yellow Cake Mix, Boxed
- vegetable oil
- eggs

Directions:

1. Supply your smoker with wood pellets and follow the start-up procedure. Preheat the grill, with the lid closed, to 350° F.

2. Pour melted butter into a 12-inch cast iron pan. Sprinkle brown sugar on top of the butter. Arrange pineapple slices on brown sugar, squeezing in as many slices as possible. Place a cherry in center of each pineapple slice; press gently into brown sugar.

3. Make cake batter as directed on box, substituting pineapple juice mixture for as much of the water as possible, and adding in required oil and eggs. Pour batter into cast iron dish, over pineapple and cherries.

4. Place the cast iron pan on the grill grate and cook for 20 minutes. Rotate the pan a half turn to ensure it cooks evenly. Cook for an additional 20 minutes, or until toothpick inserted in center comes out clean.

5. Immediately run knife around side of pan to loosen cake. Place heatproof serving plate upside down onto pan; turn plate and pan over.

6. Leave pan over cake 5 minutes so brown sugar topping can drizzle over cake. Cool 30 minutes. Enjoy!

Mint Butter Chocolate Chip Cookies

Servings: 24

Cooking Time: 12 Minutes

Ingredients:

- ➢ 1/2 Cup Butter, Melted
- ➢ 1 Package Chocolate Chip Cookie Mix
- ➢ 8-10 Drop Food Coloring
- ➢ 1/2 Tsp Mint, Extract

Directions:

1. Supply your smoker with wood pellets and follow the start-up procedure. Preheat the grill, with the lid closed, to 350° F.

2. Follow the directions on the back of the Chocolate Chip Cookie mix and also add the mint extract and green food coloring. Mix until combined.

3. On a baking sheet lined with parchment paper, drop balls of dough about 2 tbsp in size onto the pan.

4. Place in your Grill and bake for 10-12 minutes. Let cool for a couple minutes before removing from the pan. Enjoy!

Baked Irish Creme Cake

Servings: 4

Cooking Time: 60 Minutes

Ingredients:

- ➢ 1 Cup Pecans, pieces
- ➢ 1 Yellow Cake Mix, Boxed
- ➢ 1 Vanilla Pudding Mix, Instant Package (3.4oz)
- ➢ 4 Large eggs
- ➢ 1/2 Cup water
- ➢ 1/2 Cup vegetable oil
- ➢ 1 Cup Irish Cream Liquor
- ➢ 1/2 Cup butter
- ➢ 1 Cup sugar

Directions:

1. Grease and flour a 10" (25 cm) Bundt pan. Sprinkle pecans along the bottom.

2. In a large bowl, with a mixer, combine yellow cake mix, pudding mix, eggs, water, oil, and Irish Cream liquor. Pour batter over nuts in the pan.

3. Supply your smoker with wood pellets and follow the start-up procedure. Preheat the grill, with the lid closed, to 325° F.

4. Place Bundt pan on the Traeger and bake for 1 hour, or until a toothpick comes out clean. Remove from heat, cool for 10 minutes. Grill: 325 °F

5. While the cake is cooling, combine the butter, water and sugar and bring to a boil. Boil for 5 minutes, stirring constantly. Remove from heat and add Irish cream liquor.

6. Use a bamboo skewer to poke holes in the cooled cake. Spoon glaze over the cake. Allow cake to absorb the glaze. Enjoy!

Irish Soda Bread

Servings: 8-12	Cooking Time: 45 Minutes

Ingredients:

- As Needed Cornmeal
- 3 1/2 Cup all-purpose flour
- 1 1/2 Teaspoon sugar
- 1 1/4 Teaspoon baking soda
- 1 Teaspoon salt
- 1 Cup buttermilk
- To Taste butter

Directions:

1. When ready to cook, set the temperature to 400F (205 C) and preheat, lid closed, for 10 to 15 minutes.

2. Lightly dust the bottom of an 8-inch (20-cm) round cake pan with cornmeal and set aside.

3. Tear off a large sheet of wax paper and lay it on your work surface.

4. Combine the flour, sugar, soda, and salt in a large sifter and sift onto the wax paper. Carefully lift up the sides of the wax paper and tip the flour mixture back into the sifter. Re-sift into a large mixing bowl.

5. Lightly flour your work surface. Make a well in the middle of the flour mixture in the bowl and pour in 1 cup (240 mL) of buttermilk. Stir with a wooden spoon. Work quickly and gently as the carbon dioxide bubbles formed when the buttermilk hits the dry ingredients will deflate, the dough will look somewhat shaggy. If the dough seems dryish, add a little more buttermilk.

6. Turn out onto the floured surface, and with floured hands, knead gently for 10 to 20 seconds - just long enough to bring the dough bits together. (It will look more like biscuit dough than bread dough.)

7. Form into a flattish round and transfer to the prepared pan. Flour a sharp knife, and deeply cut a cross in the top of the loaf all the way to the edge of the bread. Quickly get it in to bake, if it sits too long, it will deflate.

8. Bake the bread for 45 to 50 minutes, or until it is browned and the bottom of the loaf sounds hollow when rapped with your knuckles.

9. Remove the bread from the baking pan and cool on a cooling rack. Just be-fore serving, cut the loaf in half and then slice each half into thin slices.

10. Serve with butter. Wrap leftovers tightly in plastic wrap or foil. This bread makes great toast. Enjoy!

S'mores Dip Skillet

Servings: 4-6

Cooking Time: 8 Minutes

Ingredients:

- ➤ 2 tablespoons salted butter, melted
- ➤ ¼ cup milk
- ➤ 12 ounces semisweet chocolate chips
- ➤ 16 ounces Jet-Puffed marshmallows
- ➤ Graham crackers and apple wedges, for serving

Directions:

1. Supply your smoker with wood pellets and follow the start-up procedure. Preheat, with the lid closed, to 450°F.

2. Place a cast iron skillet on the preheated grill grate and pour in the melted butter and milk, stirring for about 1 minute.

3. Once the mixture starts to heat, top with the chocolate chips in an even layer and arrange the marshmallows standing up to cover all of the chocolate.

4. Close the lid and smoke for 5 to 7 minutes, or until the marshmallows are lightly toasted.

5. Remove from the heat and serve immediately with graham crackers and apple wedges for dipping.

SEAFOOD RECIPES

Seared Ahi Tuna Steak With Soy Sauce

Servings: 2

Cooking Time: 60 Minutes

Ingredients:

- 1/2 Cup Gluten Free Soy Sauce
- 1 Large Sushi Grade Ahi Tuna Steak, Patted Dry
- 1/4 Cup Lime Juice
- 2 Tablespoons Rice Wine Vinegar
- 2 Tablespoons Sesame Oil, Divided
- 2 Tablespoons Sriracha Sauce
- 4 Tablespoons Sweet Heat Rub
- 2 Cups Water

Directions:

1. Supply your smoker with wood pellets and follow the start-up procedure. Preheat the grill, with the lid closed, to 400° F. If using gas or charcoal, set it up for high heat over direct heat.

2. In the glass baking dish, pour in the water, soy sauce, lime juice, rice wine vinegar, 1 tablespoon sesame oil, sriracha sauce, and mirin. Whisk the marinade together with the whisk until everything is well combine. Place the ahi steak into the marinade and place the glass baking dish with the ahi steak in the refrigerator for 30 minutes. After 30 minutes, flip the ahi steak over so that the ahi has the chance to fully marinate on all sides, and allow to marinate for 30 more minutes.

3. After the tuna steak has finished marinating, drain off the marinade and pat the steak dry with paper towels on all sides. Pour the Sweet Heat Rub onto the plate and rub the remaining tablespoon of sesame oil generously on all sides of the tuna steak, and then gently place the tuna steak into the seasoning on the plate, turning on all sides to coat evenly.

4. Insert a temperature probe into the thickest part of the ahi steak and place the steak on the hottest part of the grill. Grill the ahi tuna steak for 45 seconds on each side, or just until the outside is opaque and has grill marks. Flip the steak and allow it to grill for another 45 seconds until the outside is just cooked through. The ahi tuna steak's internal temperature should be just at 115°F.

5. Remove the steak from the grill once it reaches 115°F, and immediately slice and serve. The inside of the steak should still be cool and ruby pink.

Dijon-smoked Halibut

Servings: 6

Cooking Time: 120 Minutes

Ingredients:

- 4 (6-ounce) halibut steaks
- ¼ cup extra-virgin olive oil
- 2 teaspoons kosher salt
- 1 teaspoon freshly ground black pepper
- ½ cup mayonnaise
- ½ cup sweet pickle relish
- ¼ cup finely chopped sweet onion
- ¼ cup chopped roasted red pepper
- ¼ cup finely chopped tomato
- ¼ cup finely chopped cucumber
- 2 tablespoons Dijon mustard
- 1 teaspoon minced garlic

Directions:

1. Rub the halibut steaks with the olive oil and season on both sides with the salt and pepper. Transfer to a plate, cover with plastic wrap, and refrigerate for 4 hours.

2. Supply your smoker with wood pellets and follow the start-up procedure. Preheat, with the lid closed, to 200°F.

3. Remove the halibut from the refrigerator and rub with the mayonnaise.

4. Put the fish directly on the grill grate, close the lid, and smoke for 2 hours, or until opaque and an instant-read thermometer inserted in the fish reads 140°F.

5. While the fish is smoking, combine the pickle relish, onion, roasted red pepper, tomato, cucumber, Dijon mustard, and garlic in a medium bowl. Refrigerate the mustard relish until ready to serve.

6. Serve the halibut steaks hot with the mustard relish.

Barbecued Shrimp

Servings: 4

Cooking Time: 10 Minutes

Ingredients:

- 1 pound peeled and deveined shrimp, with tails on
- 2 tablespoons olive oil
- 1 batch Dill Seafood Rub

Directions:

1. Soak wooden skewers in water for 30 minutes.

2. Supply your smoker with wood pellets and follow the start-up procedure. Preheat the grill, with the lid closed, to 375°F.

3. Thread 4 or 5 shrimp per skewer.

4. Coat the shrimp all over with olive oil and season each side of the skewers with the rub.

5. Place the skewers directly on the grill grate and grill the shrimp for 5 minutes per side. Remove the skewers from the grill and serve immediately.

Grilled Garlic Shrimp With Cajun Dip

Servings: 4

Cooking Time: 15 Minutes

Ingredients:

➢ 1 Grated Garlic Cloves, Peeled

➢ 1 Tsp Lemon Juice

➢ ½ Cup Mayonnaise

➢ 2 Tbsp Olive Oil

➢ 1 ½ Tbsp Hickory Bacon Rub

➢ Scallions

➢ ½ Lb Shelled And Deveined Shrimp

➢ 1 Cup Sour Cream

Directions:

1. Supply your smoker with wood pellets and follow the start-up procedure. Preheat the grill, with the lid closed, to 350° F. If you're using a gas or charcoal grill, set it to medium heat.

2. In a glass mixing bowl, add mayonnaise, sour cream, Cajun seasoning, garlic, lemon juice, hot sauce, and Hickory Bacon. Whisk together until well combined.

3. Cajun shrimp: In a small bowl, add shrimp, olive oil, Cajun-style seasoning and Hickory Bacon seasoning and toss to combine. Set aside.

4. Transfer dip mixture into cast iron ramekin or small Dutch oven and cover with foil. Place on preheated grill and cook for 10-15 minutes, or until dip begins to bubble along the edges. At the same time, place cast iron pan on grill and add shrimp. Cook for about 3-5 minutes on each side or until shrimp are opaque.

5. Remove dip from grill and top with Cajun shrimp and scallions. Serve warm alongside garlic toast squares and enjoy!

Bacon Wrapped Scallops

Servings: 8

Cooking Time: 20 Minutes

Ingredients:

- 24 jumbo deep sea diver scallops, dry-packed
- 1/2 Cup butter
- salt
- freshly ground black pepper
- 1 Clove garlic, minced
- 12 Slices thin-cut bacon, cut in half crosswise
- lemon wedges, for serving

Directions:

1. Remove the small, crescent-shaped muscle from the side of each scallop, if still attached. Dry the scallops thoroughly on paper towels, then transfer to a medium bowl.

2. Melt butter in a small saucepan, add garlic and cook for 1 minute. Let cool slightly then pour over the scallops. Season with salt and pepper and gently toss to coat.

3. Wrap a piece of bacon around each scallop and secure with a toothpick.

4. Supply your smoker with wood pellets and follow the start-up procedure. Preheat the grill, with the lid closed, to 400° F.

5. Arrange the scallops directly on the grill grate. Grill for 15 to 20 minutes, or until the scallop is opaque and the bacon has begun to crisp. If desired, you can turn the scallops on their side, bacon-side down, turning occasionally to crisp the bacon. Do not overcook. Grill: 400 °F

6. Transfer the scallops to a platter and serve with lemon wedges.

Hot-smoked Salmon

Servings: 4	Cooking Time: 180minutes

Ingredients:

- ➢ 1½lb (680g) skinless center-cut salmon fillet, preferably wild caught
- ➢ for the brine
- ➢ 1 quart (1 liter) distilled water
- ➢ ¼ cup coarse salt
- ➢ ¼ cup light brown sugar or low-carb equivalent
- ➢ ¼ cup gin (optional)

Directions:

1. In a saucepan on the stovetop over medium-high heat, make the brine by combining the water, salt, brown sugar, and gin (if using). Bring the mixture to a boil. Stir until the salt and sugar dissolve. Remove the pan from the stovetop and let the brine cool to room temperature. Refrigerate until cool.

2. Run your fingers over the salmon fillet, feeling for bones. Remove any with kitchen tweezers or needle-nosed pliers. Rinse the salmon under cold running water. Place the salmon in a resealable plastic bag and pour the brine over it. Refrigerate for 4 to 8 hours.

3. Place a wire rack on a rimmed sheet pan. Remove the salmon from the brine and rinse under cold running water. Pat dry with paper towels and then place the salmon on the wire rack. Place the pan in a cool area with good air circulation (such as near a fan). In 2 to 4 hours, you'll notice the salmon has developed a pellicle—a kind of sticky skin or coating that will help the smoke adhere to the fish. (Don't skip this step.)

4. Supply your smoker with wood pellets and follow the start-up procedure. Preheat the grill, with the lid closed, to 150° F.

5. Place the salmon on the grate and smoke until the fish flakes easily when pressed with a fork and the internal temperature reaches 140°F (60°C), about 3 hours. If albumin (a harmless white protein) appears on top of the fillet as it smokes, gently remove it with a paper towel.

6. Remove the salmon from the grill and let rest for 10 minutes. (You can also transfer the fish to a clean wire rack and let it cool to room temperature. Cover and refrigerate if not using immediately. The salmon will keep for up to 5 days.)

7. Serve the salmon with eggs, on salads, with Mustard Caviar, or with its traditional accompaniments: cream cheese, capers, chopped hard-boiled eggs, diced red onion, and dark bread.

Thai-style Swordfish Steaks With Peanut Sauce

Servings: 4

Cooking Time: 8 Minutes

Ingredients:

- 4 center-cut swordfish steaks, each about 6oz (170g) and 1 inch (2.5cm) thick
- Peanut Sauce
- lime wedges
- for the marinade
- ½ cup light Thai-style unsweetened coconut milk
- 2 garlic cloves, peeled and smashed with a chef's knife
- juice and zest of 1 lime
- 1-inch (2.5cm) piece of fresh ginger, peeled and roughly chopped
- ½ Thai bird's eye chili pepper or serrano pepper, deseeded and thinly sliced, plus more
- 2 tbsp fresh cilantro leaves, coarsely chopped
- 1 tbsp Asian fish sauce
- 1 tbsp light soy sauce or liquid aminos
- 1 tbsp light brown sugar or low-carb substitute
- 1 tsp ground coriander
- ½ tsp ground turmeric

Directions:

1. In a medium bowl, make the marinade by whisking together the ingredients. Whisk until the brown sugar dissolves.

2. Place the swordfish steaks in a single layer in a nonreactive baking dish and pour the marinade over them, turning the steaks to coat thoroughly. Refrigerate for 1 hour.

3. Supply your smoker with wood pellets and follow the start-up procedure. Preheat the grill, with the lid closed, to 450° F.

4. Remove the swordfish from the marinade and scrape off any solids. (Discard the marinade.) Place the steaks on the grate and grill until the fish easily flakes when pressed with a fork, about 3 to 4 minutes per side, turning with a thin-bladed spatula.

5. Transfer the swordfish steaks to a platter. Serve with the peanut sauce and lime wedges.

Honey-soy Garlic Salmon

Servings: 4

Cooking Time: 6 Minutes

Ingredients:

- ➢ 1 Tsp Chili Paste
- ➢ Chives, Chopped
- ➢ 2 Grate Garlic, Cloves
- ➢ 2 Tbsp Minced Ginger, Fresh
- ➢ 1 Tsp Honey
- ➢ 2 Tbsp Lemon, Juice
- ➢ 4 Salmon, Fillets (Skin Removed)
- ➢ 1 Tsp Sesame Oil
- ➢ 2 Tbsp Soy Sauce, Low Sodium

Directions:

1. Supply your smoker with wood pellets and follow the start-up procedure. Preheat the grill, with the lid closed, to 400° F.

2. Take the salmon and place it in a large resealable plastic bag, and then top with all remaining ingredients, except the chives. Seal the plastic bag and toss evenly to coat the salmon. Marinade in the refrigerator for 20 minutes.

3. After the salmon has been marinading for 20 minutes, place salmon on a flat pan or right on the grates and grill for about 3 minutes, and then flip and grill on the second side for about 3 minutes. Turn off the Grill, remove the pan from grill, plate, garnish with chives, and enjoy!

Grilled Trout With Citrus & Basil

Servings: 4

Cooking Time: 10 Minutes

Ingredients:

- ➢ 6 Whole Trout
- ➢ 2 Teaspoon Blackened Saskatchewan Rub
- ➢ 10 Sprig fresh basil
- ➢ 2 Lemons, cut in half
- ➢ extra-virgin olive oil

Directions:

1. Supply your smoker with wood pellets and follow the start-up procedure. Preheat the grill, with the lid closed, to 450° F.

2. Season the center cavity of the trout with the Traeger Blackened Saskatchewan. Place two sprigs of Basil in each cavity, then add 4 lemon halves.

3. Next tie the fish closed using the Butchers twine, and then rub with olive oil.

4. Place the trout on the hot grill and cook 5 minutes on each side. Enjoy! Grill: 450 ˚F

Cold-smoked Salmon Gravlax

Servings: 6

Cooking Time: 30 Minutes

Ingredients:

- 1 Cup kosher salt
- 1 Cup sugar
- 1 Tablespoon freshly ground black pepper
- 2 Pound Sushi-Grad Salmon Fillet, Skin-on, Pin Bones Removed
- 2 Bunch Dill Weed, fresh
- capers, drained
- red onion, sliced
- cream cheese
- lemons

Directions:

1. In a bowl stir together the salt, sugar and black pepper until thoroughly combined. On a work surface, turn salmon skin side up and sprinkle about half of salt mixture all over and rub in.

2. Arrange half the dill on the bottom of a baking dish large enough to hold the salmon. Set salmon skin side down on bed of dill.

3. Rub remaining salt mixture all over top and sides of salmon, then top with remaining dill. Cover with plastic, then top with a weight on a smaller baking dish or a plate with cans of beans on top, then place in refrigerator and allow to cure for 2 days.

4. Remove salmon from refrigerator, rinse under cold water and pat dry with paper towels. Allow to sit at room temperature on the counter for 1 hour

5. Supply your smoker with wood pellets and follow the start-up procedure. Preheat the grill, with the lid closed, to 180° F. Place salmon onto a baking pan. Fill another baking pan with ice and place baking pan with salmon over ice. Place onto grill and smoke for 30 minutes.

6. Remove from grill and slice thin. Serve with capers, red onion, dill, cream cheese, and lemon. Enjoy!

Grilled Fresh Fish

Servings: 2

Cooking Time: 15 Minutes

Ingredients:

➢ 1 Whole fillet of firm white fish: sea bass, halibut or cod

➢ Fin & Feather Rub

➢ 2 Whole lemons

Directions:

1. Supply your smoker with wood pellets and follow the start-up procedure. Preheat the grill, with the lid closed, to 325° F.

2. Season fish with Traeger Fin & Feather Rub and let sit for 30 minutes. Slice lemons in half.

3. Place the fish and the lemons (cut side down) directly on the grill grates. Cook for 10 to 15 minutes until the fish is flaky and is at least 145°F in the thickest part of fish. Be careful not to over cook.

4. Serve with the grilled lemons. Enjoy!

Grilled Lemon Lobster Tails

Servings: 3

Cooking Time: 7 Minutes

Ingredients:

➢ 6 lobster tails

➢ 1/4 cup melted butter

➢ 1/4 cup fresh lemon juice

➢ 1 tablespoon fresh dill

➢ 1 teaspoon salt

➢ 6 lime wedges

Directions:

1. Supply your smoker with wood pellets and follow the start-up procedure. Preheat the grill, with the lid closed, to 375° F.

2. Split the lobster tails in half place then back side down.

3. Cut down through the center to the shell the whole length of each tail.

4. Pull the shell back, exposing the meat.

5. Pat the lobster tails with paper towel to dry.

6. Combine in a small mixing bowl the butter, lemon juice, dill, and salt until the salt has dissolved.

7. Brush the mixture onto the flesh side of each lobster tail.

8. Place the lobster tails onto the grill and cook for 5 to 7 minutes, turning them once during the cooking process. (The shells should turn a bright pink).

9. Remove the heat.

10. Serve with lime wedges!

Grilled Garlic Lobster Tails

Servings: 2

Cooking Time: 11 Minutes

Ingredients:

- 4 Lobster Tails (8 oz Each)
- 3 Sticks Unsalted Butter
- 4 Cloves Garlic Minced
- ½ Cup Fresh Parsley Chopped
- Juice of 1 Lemon
- 2 Tablespoons Fresh Lemon Zest
- 2 Teaspoons Crushed Red Pepper
- ¼ Cup Olive Oil
- 1 TBS Kosher Salt
- 1 TBS Cracked Black Pepper

Directions:

1. Supply your smoker with wood pellets and follow the start-up procedure. Preheat the grill, with the lid closed, to 375° F.

2. Split lobster tails in half lengthwise and season with salt, pepper, and olive oil.

3. Place butter in an aluminum pan and put the pan on the hot side of the grill to melt the butter.

4. Add garlic, parsley, lemon zest, lemon juice, and red pepper to butter and simmer for 5 minutes.

5. Place lobster tails meat side down on the grill and cook for 6 minutes. Baste the shell side with the butter mixture.

6. Dunk each tail in the butter mixture and then transfer to the grill, shell side down. Baste meat again with butter mixture.

7. Cook for an additional 5 minutes or until the lobster meat turns opaque and shells are bright pink.

8. Serve with remaining butter mixture, fresh parsley, and lemon wedges.

PORK RECIPES

Bbq Pork Shoulder Steaks

Servings: 4

Cooking Time: 120 Minutes

Ingredients:

- 4 (1 to 1-1/4 inch thick) pork shoulder steaks
- 1/2 Cup mustard
- Pork & Poultry Rub
- 1/2 Cup apple juice
- 1 Cup 'Que BBQ Sauce

Directions:

1. Slather the pork steaks on all sides with the mustard and season with the Traeger Pork & Poultry Rub. (The mustard will help keep the pork moist, but the taste will be unnoticeable in the final product.)

2. Supply your smoker with wood pellets and follow the start-up procedure. Preheat the grill, with the lid closed, to 180° F.

3. Arrange the steaks on the grill grate. Smoke for 1-1/2 hours. Grill: 180 °F

4. Remove the pork steaks to a plate and increase temperature to 225°F. Preheat 5 to 10 minutes. Grill: 225 °F

5. Meanwhile, wrap each steak with aluminum foil, adding in a couple tablespoons of apple juice.

6. Cook the steaks for another hour or so or until they are tender (about 160°F on an instant-read meat thermometer). Grill: 225 °F Probe: 160 °F

7. The last 15 minutes, take the pork steaks out of the foil and put them directly on the grill.

8. Brush each steak on both sides with the Traeger 'Que BBQ Sauce or your favorite barbecue sauce.

9. Let the steaks rest for 3 minutes before serving. Enjoy!

Pork Belly Burnt Ends

Servings: 8-10

Cooking Time: 360 Minutes

Ingredients:

➢ 1 (3-pound) skinless pork belly (if not already skinned, use a sharp boning knife to remove the skin from the belly), cut into 1½- to 2-inch cubes

➢ 1 batch Sweet Brown Sugar Rub

➢ ½ cup honey

➢ 1 cup The Ultimate BBQ Sauce

➢ 2 tablespoons light brown sugar

Directions:

1. Supply your smoker with wood pellets and follow the start-up procedure. Preheat the grill, with the lid closed, to 250°F.

2. Generously season the pork belly cubes with the rub. Using your hands, work the rub into the meat.

3. Place the pork cubes directly on the grill grate and smoke until their internal temperature reaches 195°F.

4. Transfer the cubes from the grill to an aluminum pan. Add the honey, barbecue sauce, and brown sugar. Stir to combine and coat the pork.

5. Place the pan in the grill and smoke the pork for 1 hour, uncovered. Remove the pork from the grill and serve immediately.

Bangers And Potato Mash

Servings: 6 - 8

Cooking Time: 135 Minutes

Ingredients:

- Bbq Sauce
- ¼ Cup Butter
- 3 Garlic, Cloves
- 1 Onion, Chopped
- 8 Red Potatoes, Medium
- 8 Sausages, Pork
- ½ Cup Milk

Directions:

1. Using a fork, poke holes all over every red potato.

2. Cut a whole bulb of garlic in half and set aside.

3. Supply your smoker with wood pellets and follow the start-up procedure. Preheat the grill, with the lid open, to 300° F.

4. Set the halved garlic bulb and red potatoes on the grill. Cook the garlic for 30 minutes and the potatoes for 75 minutes.

5. Turn your down to 250°F and allow it to settle to that temperature.

6. Peel and mash the potatoes and garlic with butter and milk until the desired smoothness is achieved.

7. Set the sausages on the grill and smoke for 1 hour.

8. Sauté sliced onions in a pan with butter and barbecue sauce to taste.

9. After 1 hour, remove the sausages and turn off the grill. Place the onions on top of the mash potatoes and the sausage on top of the onions. Add more BBQ sauce if you wish.

Baked Maple And Brown Sugar Bacon

Servings: 4

Cooking Time: 60 Minutes

Ingredients:

➢ 1 Pound cold bacon

➢ 1/2 Cup pure maple syrup, warmed

➢ 1/2 Cup brown sugar, plus more as needed

Directions:

1. Supply your smoker with wood pellets and follow the start-up procedure. Preheat the grill, with the lid closed, to 300° F.

2. Line a rimmed baking sheet with foil and place a wire rack on top. Lay bacon strips in a single layer on the wire rack.

3. Using a pastry brush, brush each strip of bacon on both sides with the warmed maple syrup, then sprinkle brown sugar evenly on both sides.

4. Put the baking sheet in the grill and cook bacon for 60-75 minutes, or until bacon browns and appears to be crisping. Grill: 300 ˚F

5. Allow the bacon to cool slightly before eating. Enjoy!

Sweet Bacon

Servings: 4

Cooking Time: 60 Minutes

Ingredients:

- ➢ 1 Pack Bacon, Thick Cut
- ➢ 1/2 Cup Brown Sugar
- ➢ 1/2 Cup Maple Syrup
- ➢ Mandarin Habanero Seasoning

Directions:

1. Place the bacon in a deep dish. Add the maple syrup, cover and refrigerate 2 - 3 hours or overnight.

2. Supply your smoker with wood pellets and follow the start-up procedure. Preheat the grill, with the lid open, to 225° F.

3. When the grill has preheated, place the bacon directly on the cooking grids and sprinkle with brown sugar and Mandarin Habanero. Check every 15-20. After 30 minutes, flip and rotate bacon and baste with syrup. Allow to hot smoke for another 20 to 30 minutes or until the bacon is done to your desired liking.

4. Allow to cool on a rack and serve.

5. Can be refrigerated in an airtight container.

Grilled German Sausage With A Smoky Delicious Twist

Servings: 8

Cooking Time: 120 Minutes

Ingredients:

- ➢ 2 Tablespoon Jacobsen Salt Co. Pure Kosher Sea Salt
- ➢ 1 Teaspoon The Sausage Maker Instacure #1
- ➢ 1 Tablespoon ground nutmeg
- ➢ 2 Teaspoon ground mace
- ➢ 1 Teaspoon ground ginger
- ➢ 4 Pound ground pork, 80% lean
- ➢ 1 Pound ground veal or ground beef
- ➢ 2 Large eggs
- ➢ 1 Cup nonfat dry milk powder

Directions:

1. Combine salt, Instacure #1, nutmeg, mace and ginger in a large pitcher or small bowl. Add the milk and eggs. Beat until well combined. Pour the egg mixture over the ground meat and mix gently. Using your hands, mix in the milk powder until evenly distributed.

2. Form the meat into sausage links, roughly 4 to 6 inches in length.

3. Supply your smoker with wood pellets and follow the start-up procedure. Preheat the grill, with the lid closed, to 225° F.

4. Smoke for approximately 2 hours, or until the internal temperature reaches 175°F. Serve immediately or refrigerate until ready to serve. Enjoy! Grill: 225 ˚F Probe: 175 ˚F

Pork Tenderloin With Bourbon Peaches

Servings: 6   Cooking Time: 27 Minutes

Ingredients:

- 2 pork tenderloins, about 2lb (1kg) total, trimmed of silver skin and excess fat
- extra virgin olive oil
- for the rub
- 3 tbsp coarse salt
- 3 tbsp freshly ground black pepper
- 3 tbsp smoked or regular paprika
- 3 tbsp granulated light brown sugar or low-carb substitute
- 2 tbsp instant coffee
- 1 tbsp granulated garlic
- 2 tsp ground cumin
- 1 tsp chili powder
- for the peaches
- 4 freestone peaches, about 1lb (450g) total, peeled, pitted, and sliced
- 1 tbsp freshly squeezed lemon juice
- ¼ cup unsalted butter
- 4 tbsp granulated light brown sugar or low-carb substitute
- 2 tbsp bourbon
- ½ tsp ground cinnamon
- ½ tsp pure vanilla extract
- pinch of coarse salt

Directions:

1. Supply your smoker with wood pellets and follow the start-up procedure. Preheat the grill, with the lid closed, to 400° F.

2. In a small bowl, make the rub by combining the ingredients. Coat the tenderloins in olive oil and season with the rub.

3. Place the peaches and lemon juice in a medium bowl, turning the peaches gently to coat. Measure the other ingredients and then take them and the peaches grill side.

4. Place 1 tablespoon of olive oil in the hot skillet and add the tenderloins. Quickly sear the pork, about 2 to 3 minute per side, turning as needed with tongs. When they're nicely browned, transfer the tenderloins to the grate. Cook until the internal temperature in the thickest part of the meat reaches 145°F (63°C), about 8 minutes. For moist meat, don't cook the tenderloins beyond 155°F (68°C).

5. Transfer the pork to a cutting board and tent with aluminum foil.

6. Replace the cast iron skillet with a clean one and close the grill lid to let it heat. Once hot, make the bourbon peaches by melting the butter. Add the brown sugar, bourbon, cinnamon, vanilla, and salt. Cook the mixture until it bubbles, about 5 to 8 minutes. Add the peaches and cook for 5 to 8 minutes more, turning the peaches carefully with a spoon to coat. Carefully transfer the skillet to a trivet or another heatproof surface.

7. Slice the pork on a diagonal into ½-inch (1.25cm) slices. Shingle the slices on a platter. Spoon the peaches around the pork or serve separately.

Smoked Pork Tomato Tamales

Servings: 6-8   Cooking Time: 60 Minutes

Ingredients:

- 1 Boneless, Netted Pork Roast
- 1 Cup, Fresh Cilantro, Chopped
- 3 Cloves Garlic, Peeled
- 20 Dried Cornhusks
- 1 Tbsp Lime Juice
- ¼ Cup Olive Oil
- 1 Onion, Quartered
- 4 - 6 Cups Prepared Masa Harina Tamale Dough
- 3 – 4 Serrano Peppers, Deseeded
- 1 Tbsp Sweet Heat Rub
- 1 Lb. Tomatillos, Husked And Washed

Directions:

1. Began by soaking the corn husks in a pan filled with water. Soak for 2 – 4 hours, or if needed, overnight.

2. Unwrap the tomatillos from their shell and place all of them into a grill basket followed by a few Serranos, deseeded, garlic cloves and 1 onion cut into quarters.

3. Supply your smoker with wood pellets and follow the start-up procedure. Preheat the grill, with the lid open, to 400° F. If you're using a gas or charcoal grill, set it up for medium low heat, and use smoke chips to fill your grill with smoke for 15 minutes. Place the grill basket filled with your vegetables and roast them over an open flame on your smoker until vegetables have become charred.

4. Place tomatillos, peppers, garlic and onions in a bowl, cover with plastic wrap, and let stand until cool enough to handle, 10 to 15 minutes.

5. Season the pork roast generously with Sweet Heat Rub and grill at 350°F for 1 hour until the roast has a nice crust on the outside.

6. While the pork roast is cooking, add a handful of cilantro, charred vegetables, 1 tbsp of Sweet Heat Rub, 1 tbsp lime juice, and ¼ cup of olive oil to a food processor. Pulse in food processor until mixture is consistent. Set aside

7. After the pork roast has been grilled for an hour, turn heat down to 275°F. Put roast in pan with about a cup of water, cover with aluminum foil and cook for another 4 hours or until the roast can be shredded. Pour chile verde sauce over shredded pork and toss to combine.

8. To being assembling tamales, place a corn husk on a work surface. Place 2-3 tablespoons of tamale dough on larger end of husk and spread into a rectangle, about ¼" thick, leaving a small border along the edge. Place large tablespoon of chili and pork filling on top of dough. Fold over sides of husk so dough

surrounds filling, then fold bottom of husk up and secure closed by tying a thin strip of husk around tamale.

9. To cook tamales, place them in a large metal colander over a large stockpot filled with water. Cover and let steam for 1 hour. After the tamales have been steamed, take them off and grill them at 350°F for about 10-20 minutes until corn husks have charred marks.

Grilled Sweet Pork Tenderloin

Servings: 4

Cooking Time: 20 Minutes

Ingredients:

- ➢ 2 Tablespoons Brown Sugar
- ➢ 2 Tablespoons Olive Oil
- ➢ 2 Tablespoons   Tennessee Apple Butter Seasoning
- ➢ 1 Pork Tenderloin, Trimmed With Silver Skins Removed

Directions:

1. In a small bowl, combine the olive oil, brown sugar, and Tennessee Apple Butter seasoning until well combined. Generously rub the pork tenderloin with the mixture. Allow the pork tenderloin to marinade for 1 hour.

2. Supply your smoker with wood pellets and follow the start-up procedure. Preheat the grill, with the lid open, to 350° F.

3. Grill the tenderloin for 5-7 minutes on each side, flipping the tenderloin only once and cooking until the internal temperature reaches 140-145°F.

4. Remove the tenderloin from the grill and allow to rest 10 minutes before slicing and serving.

Smoked Ham

Servings: 12-15

Cooking Time: 300 Minutes

Ingredients:

- ➢ 1 (10-pound) fresh ham, skin removed
- ➢ 2 tablespoons olive oil
- ➢ 1 batch Rosemary-Garlic Lamb Seasoning

Directions:

1. Supply your smoker with wood pellets and follow the start-up procedure. Preheat the grill, with the lid closed, to 180°F.

2. Rub the ham all over with olive oil and sprinkle it with the seasoning.

3. Place the ham directly on the grill grate and smoke for 3 hours.

4. Increase the grill's temperature to 375°F and continue to smoke the ham until its internal temperature reaches 170°F.

5. Remove the ham from the grill and let it rest for 10 minutes, before carving and serving.

Mini Sausage Rolls

Servings: 4

Cooking Time: 25 Minutes

Ingredients:

- 3/4 Cup dry mustard
- 3/4 Cup distilled white vinegar
- 1/2 Cup honey
- 4 egg yolk, beaten
- 2 Pound Sausage, Uncooked
- ground sage
- 1 Small onion, diced small
- 17 1/2 Ounce frozen puff pastry

Directions:

1. Make the mustard: Combine the mustard and vinegar in a small mixing bowl. Cover with plastic wrap and let sit overnight at room temperature to develop the flavors. Transfer the mustard mixture to a small heavy saucepan and add the honey and egg yolks. Cook over low heat, whisking constantly, until thickened, about 7 minutes. Cool, then refrigerate until serving time.

2. In a medium mixing bowl, thoroughly combine the sausage and onion. On a lightly floured work surface, roll each sheet of thawed puff pastry - there are two to a package - into an 11 by 10-1/2 inch rectangle.

3. Using a pizza cutter or knife, cut each rectangle widthwise into three strips, each 3-1/2 inches wide. Wet your hands and mold some of the sausage into a tube-like shape. Lay it down the center of one of the puff pastry strips.

4. Wrap the pastry around the sausage and seal the seams with a bit of beaten egg. Repeat with the remaining sausage and puff pastry. Put all the rolls seam side down on your work surface and brush the tops lightly with the egg.

5. Cut the rolls into pieces about 1-1/2 inches long and transfer to a rimmed baking sheet lined with parchment paper. Leave about an inch between each roll. Supply your smoker with wood pellets and follow the start-up procedure. Preheat the grill, with the lid closed, to 350° F.

6. Bake the sausage rolls for about 25 minutes, or until the sausage is cooked through and the pastry is golden brown. Serve hot with the honey mustard. Grill: 350 ˚F

Beer Braised Pork Belly And Beef

Servings: 4

Cooking Time: 90 Minutes

Ingredients:

- 1, Dark Beer, Any Brand
- 3 Cups Broth, Beef
- 1 Tablespoon Chinese Cooking Wine (Such As Shaoxing) Or Dry Sherry Wine
- 1 Teaspoon Chinese Five Spice Powder
- 2, Smashed Garlic, Cloves
- 1 Inch Knob Ginger, Peeled And Thinly Sliced
- 1 Onion, Sliced
- 2 Pounds Pork Belly, Cut Into 1 Inch Chunks
- 2 Tablespoons Rice Wine Vinegar
- 2 Tablespoons, Dark Soy Sauce, Low Sodium
- 3 Tablespoons Sugar

Directions:

1. Place a heavy dutch oven on a stovetop over medium high heat. Add the pork belly and brown on all sides, about 5 minutes. Once the pork belly has browned, add in the onion, ginger, and garlic, and stir well.

2. Pour the beer, beef broth, soy sauce, dark soy sauce, sugar, Chinese cooking wine, rice wine vinegar, and Chinese five spice powder into the pan. Place a lid on the pan and bring it to a boil. Once it boils, remove it from the heat.

3. Supply your smoker with wood pellets and follow the start-up procedure. Preheat the grill, with the lid open, to 325° F. Place the pan of pork belly on the grill and braise for 1 ½ hours, or until the pork belly is falling apart tender and glazed.

4. Remove the pork belly from the grill and serve immediately.

Grilled Prosciutto Wrapped Asparagus

Servings: 6

Cooking Time: 15 Minutes

Ingredients:

- 2 Bunch asparagus
- 4 Ounce prosciutto
- olive oil
- salt and pepper
- 1 Medium lemon, zested
- 2 Tablespoon balsamic vinegar, divided
- 3 Tablespoon toasted pine nuts, for serving

Directions:

1. Supply your smoker with wood pellets and follow the start-up procedure. Preheat the grill, with the lid closed, to 400° F.

2. Rinse the asparagus and pat dry with a paper towel. Cut the bottom third off of the asparagus stalks and discard.

3. Wrap a piece of prosciutto around 4 to 5 stalks, and place on a baking sheet. Drizzle the asparagus with olive oil, then sprinkle with salt, pepper and lemon zest.

4. Place the baking sheet on the grill and cook. After 5 minutes, shake the pan to turn the asparagus once, then drizzle with 1 tablespoon balsamic vinegar. Grill: 400 ˚F

5. Place back on the grill and cook until the prosciutto is crispy and the asparagus is cooked through, about 5 to 8 minutes. Grill: 400 ˚F

6. Place the asparagus on the serving tray and sprinkle with the pine nuts and drizzle with remaining balsamic. Enjoy!

VEGETABLES RECIPES

Roasted Jalapeno Cheddar Deviled Eggs

Servings: 6

Cooking Time: 30 Minutes

Ingredients:

- 7 Eggs, hard boiled
- 3 Tablespoon mayonnaise
- 1 Teaspoon brown mustard
- 1 Teaspoon apple cider vinegar
- 1 Dash hot sauce
- 1 jalapeño pepper, seeded and minced
- salt and pepper
- 1/2 Cup shredded cheddar cheese
- paprika

Directions:

1. Supply your smoker with wood pellets and follow the start-up procedure. Preheat the grill, with the lid closed, to 180° F.

2. Place your eggs directly on the grill grate and smoke for 30 minutes.

3. Remove from the grill and allow the eggs to cool. Smoking the eggs will give them a slightly yellowed color, but an intense smoky flavor. If a classic white egg is your preference, then skip this step.

4. Slice the eggs lengthwise and scoop the egg yolks directly into a gallon zip top bag.

5. Add the mayo, mustard, vinegar, hot sauce, roasted jalapeños and salt and pepper to the bag.

6. Zip the bag closed and, using your hands, knead all of the ingredients together in the bag until completely smooth.

7. Squeeze the yolk mixture into one corner of the bag and then cut the corner off. Pipe the yolk mixture into the whites.

8. Sprinkle with the finely shredded cheddar or paprika and chill until you are ready to serve. Enjoy!

Red Potato Grilled Lollipops

Servings: 4

Cooking Time: 25 Minutes

Ingredients:

- ➢ 8 Large red bliss potatoes, halved
- ➢ 2 Clove garlic, minced
- ➢ 2 Sprig rosemary, minced
- ➢ 2 Tablespoon olive oil
- ➢ 1 Teaspoon salt
- ➢ 1/2 Teaspoon black pepper
- ➢ 5 Wooden Skewers, soaked in water
- ➢ 1/4 Cup Parmesan cheese, grated

Directions:

1. Supply your smoker with wood pellets and follow the start-up procedure. Preheat the grill, with the lid closed, to 450° F.

2. Halve potatoes and poke each several times with a fork.

3. Put the potatoes in a large bowl and toss with the minced garlic, rosemary leaves, a few tablespoons of olive oil, kosher salt, and pepper. Microwave the potatoes for 4 minutes. Gently toss potatoes and microwave for another 3 minutes.

4. Skewer potato halves threading about 4 or 5 potato halves on each skewer. Brush potatoes with olive oil.

5. Place the potato skewers on the Traeger, cut side down, and grill until the sides begin to brown (4-7 minutes).

6. Flip and grill skin side down for another 7-10 minutes.

7. They are done when a sharp knife tip easily penetrates the sides. Remove potatoes from grill and top with grated parmesan cheese. Enjoy!

Grilled Asparagus & Honey-glazed Carrots

Servings: 4

Cooking Time: 35 Minutes

Ingredients:

- ➢ 1 Bunch asparagus, woody ends removed
- ➢ 1 Pound Carrots, peeled
- ➢ 2 Tablespoon olive oil
- ➢ sea salt
- ➢ 2 Tablespoon honey
- ➢ lemon zest

Directions:

1. Rinse all vegetables under cold water. Drizzle asparagus with olive oil and a generous sprinkling of sea salt. Generously drizzle carrots with honey and lightly sprinkle with sea salt.

2. Supply your smoker with wood pellets and follow the start-up procedure. Preheat the grill, with the lid closed, to 350° F.

3. Place carrots on the grill first and cook for 10-15 minutes, then add asparagus and cook both for another 15 to 20 minutes, or until they're done to your liking. Grill: 350 °F

4. Top the asparagus with some fresh lemon zest. Enjoy!

Blt Pasta Salad

Servings: 6

Cooking Time: 45 Minutes

Ingredients:

➢ 1 pound thick-cut bacon

➢ 16 ounces bowtie pasta, cooked according to package directions and drained

➢ 2 tomatoes, chopped

➢ ½ cup chopped scallions

➢ ½ cup Italian dressing

➢ ½ cup ranch dressing

➢ 1 tablespoon chopped fresh basil

➢ 1 teaspoon salt

➢ 1 teaspoon freshly ground black pepper

➢ 1 teaspoon garlic powder

➢ 1 head lettuce, cored and torn

Directions:

1. Supply your smoker with wood pellets and follow the start-up procedure. Preheat, with the lid closed, to 225°F.

2. Arrange the bacon slices on the grill grate, close the lid, and cook for 30 to 45 minutes, flipping after 20 minutes, until crisp.

3. Remove the bacon from the grill and chop.

4. In a large bowl, combine the chopped bacon with the cooked pasta, tomatoes, scallions, Italian dressing, ranch dressing, basil, salt, pepper, and garlic powder. Refrigerate until ready to serve.

5. Toss in the lettuce just before serving to keep it from wilting.

Roasted Green Beans With Bacon

Servings: 4

Cooking Time: 20 Minutes

Ingredients:

- ➢ 1 1/2 Pound green beans, ends trimmed
- ➢ 4 Strips bacon, cut into small pieces
- ➢ 4 Tablespoon extra-virgin olive oil
- ➢ 2 Clove garlic, minced
- ➢ 1 Teaspoon kosher salt

Directions:

1. Supply your smoker with wood pellets and follow the start-up procedure. Preheat the grill, with the lid closed, to 350° F.

2. Toss all ingredients together and spread out evenly on a sheet tray.

3. Place the tray directly on the grill grate and roast until the bacon is crispy and beans are lightly browned, about 20 minutes. Enjoy! Grill: 450 ˚F

Grilled Zucchini Squash Spears

Servings: 4

Cooking Time: 10 Minutes

Ingredients:

- ➤ 4 Medium zucchini
- ➤ 2 Tablespoon olive oil
- ➤ 1 Tablespoon sherry vinegar
- ➤ 2 thyme, leaves pulled
- ➤ salt and pepper

Directions:

1. Clean the zucchini and cut the ends off. Cut each in half lengthwise, then each half into thirds.

2. Combine remaining ingredients in a medium Ziplock bag and add the spears. Toss and mix well to coat the zucchini.

3. Supply your smoker with wood pellets and follow the start-up procedure. Preheat the grill, with the lid closed, to 350° F.

4. Remove the spears from the bag and place directly on the grill grate cut side down.

5. Cook for 3-4 minutes per side, until grill marks appear and zucchini is tender. Grill: 350 ˚F

6. Remove from grill and finish with more thyme leaves if desired. Enjoy!

Roasted Artichokes With Garlic Butter

Servings: 2

Cooking Time: 60 Minutes

Ingredients:

- 2 Large artichokes
- 3 Tablespoon olive oil
- sea salt
- 1 Stick unsalted butter
- 2 Clove garlic, chopped
- 2 Tablespoon chives, parsley, tarragon or cilantro
- 1 lemon

Directions:

1.   Supply your smoker with wood pellets and follow the start-up procedure. Preheat the grill, with the lid closed, to 375° F.

2.   Meanwhile, break off and discard any small outer leaves on the artichokes. Use a knife to slice off the tops of the artichokes, then using scissors, cut off any thorns on the remaining artichoke leaves. Trim the very bottom of the stem, then peel the tough and fibrous outer layer of the stem. Finally, cut artichokes in half and rinse off.

3.   Transfer artichokes to a large mixing bowl, drizzle with olive oil and generously sprinkle with sea salt. Toss to coat the artichokes thoroughly. Grill: 375 ℉

4.   Add the artichokes to the grill, cut side down, and roast at 375℉ until the artichoke bottoms are tender when poked with a fork or knife, about 50 to 60 minutes. Grill: 375 ℉

5.   When artichokes are almost done, add butter, chopped garlic and a pinch of sea salt to a small sauce pan and melt slowly over medium-low heat. Once the butter melts all the way and starts to bubble slightly, add the herbs.

6.   When the artichokes are done, transfer to a butcher paper lined tray with the cut sides up. Drizzle half the garlic butter and squeeze half of the lemon over the artichokes. Add a small sprinkle of sea salt over the artichokes.

7.   Serve with a ramekin of the remaining butter for dipping and extra wedges of lemon. Enjoy! Chef Tip: You can also serve with a ramekin of good mayonnaise mixed with a bit of hot sauce.

Grilled Asparagus And Hollandaise Sauce

Servings: 4

Cooking Time: 10 Minutes

Ingredients:

- ➢ 1 Pound asparagus
- ➢ 2 Teaspoon red pepper flakes
- ➢ 2 Tablespoon olive oil
- ➢ salt and pepper
- ➢ 4 egg yolk
- ➢ 1 Tablespoon lemon juice
- ➢ 1/2 Cup butter, melted
- ➢ cayenne pepper
- ➢ salt

Directions:

1. Supply your smoker with wood pellets and follow the start-up procedure. Preheat the grill, with the lid closed, to 375° F.

2. In a large bowl, mix asparagus with olive oil, red pepper flakes and salt. Arrange asparagus on a cooking sheet and take to the grill. Cook for approximately 10 to 15 minutes. Grill: 375 °F

3. In an aluminum bowl, whisk the egg yolks well. Add the lemon juice and whisk until creamy.

4. Place bowl over a double boiler, over low heat, making sure that it does not touches the water.

5. While whisking, add the melted butter slowly. Whisk until it doubles the volume. Take off the heat, still whisking and add the cayenne pepper and salt.

6. Arrange asparagus over a serving plater. Pour hollandaise sauce over asparagus and serve. Enjoy!

Baked Winter Squash Au Gratin

Servings: 8

Cooking Time: 45 Minutes

Ingredients:

- ➢ 2 Cup heavy cream
- ➢ salt and pepper
- ➢ 3 Cup shredded Gruyere cheese
- ➢ 4 Clove garlic, diced
- ➢ 2 Tablespoon butter
- ➢ 3 yellow potatoes, peeled and cubed
- ➢ 1 butternut squash seeded, peeled and cubed
- ➢ 1 acorn squash seeded, peeled and cubed

Directions:

1. Supply your smoker with wood pellets and follow the start-up procedure. Preheat the grill, with the lid closed, to 375° F.

2. In a medium saucepan, cook the cream, stirring constantly, until it comes to a low boil. Add salt, pepper, garlic and shredded Gruyere cheese. Stir until cheese is melted.

3. Grease a 9x13 inch baking dish with 2 tablespoons of butter. In a large mixing bowl, combine potatoes, butternut and acorn squash. Stir in the cheese sauce. Place mixture in the prepared baking dish and place in grill.

4. Cook for 45 minutes or until potatoes and squash are fork tender. Remove from grill and let cool for 10 minutes before serving. Enjoy! Grill: 375 °F

Baked Breakfast Mini Quiches

Servings: 8

Cooking Time: 15 Minutes

Ingredients:

- cooking spray
- 1 Tablespoon extra-virgin olive oil
- 1/2 yellow onion, diced
- 3 Cup Spinach, fresh
- 10 eggs
- 4 Ounce shredded cheddar, mozzarella or Swiss cheese
- 1/4 Cup fresh basil
- 1 Teaspoon kosher salt
- 1/2 Teaspoon black pepper

Directions:

1. Spray a 12-cup muffin tin generously with cooking spray.

2. In a small skillet over medium heat, warm the oil. Add the onion and cook, stirring frequently, until softened, about 7 minutes. Add the spinach and cook until wilted, about 1 minute longer.

3. Transfer to a cutting board to cool, then chop the mixture so the spinach if broken up a little.

4. Supply your smoker with wood pellets and follow the start-up procedure. Preheat the grill, with the lid closed, to 350° F.

5. In a large bowl, whisk the eggs until frothy. Add the cooled onions and spinach, cheese, basil, 1 tsp salt and 1/2 tsp pepper. Stir to combine. Divide egg mixture evenly among the muffin cups.

6. Place tray on the grill and bake until the eggs have puffed up, are set, and are beginning to brown, about 18 to 20 minutes. Grill: 350 ˚F

7. Serve immediately, or allow to cool on a wire rack, then refrigerate in an air tight container for up to 4 days. Enjoy!

Roasted Sweet Potato Steak Fries

Servings: 4

Cooking Time: 40 Minutes

Ingredients:

- ➢ 3 Whole sweet potatoes
- ➢ 4 Tablespoon extra-virgin olive oil
- ➢ salt and pepper
- ➢ 2 Tablespoon fresh chopped rosemary

Directions:

1. Supply your smoker with wood pellets and follow the start-up procedure. Preheat the grill, with the lid closed, to 450° F.

2. Cut sweet potatoes into wedges and toss with olive oil, salt, pepper and rosemary. Spread on a parchment lined baking sheet and put in the grill. Cook for 15 minutes then flip and continue to cook until lightly browned and cooked through, about 40 to 45 minutes total. Grill: 450 ˚F

3. Serve with your favorite dipping sauce. Enjoy! Grill: 450 ˚F

Mashed Red Potatoes

Servings: 4

Cooking Time: 40 Minutes

Ingredients:

- 8 Large red potatoes
- salt
- black pepper
- 1/2 Cup heavy cream
- 1/4 Cup butter

Directions:

1. Supply your smoker with wood pellets and follow the start-up procedure. Preheat the grill, with the lid closed, to 180° F.

2. Slice red potatoes in half, lengthwise then cut in half again to make quarters. Season potatoes with salt and pepper.

3. Increase the heat to High and preheat. Once the grill is hot, set potatoes directly on the grill grate. Grill: 450 ˚F

4. Every 15 minutes flip potatoes to ensure all sides get color. Continue to do this until potatoes are fork tender.

5. When tender, mash potatoes with cream, butter, salt, and pepper to taste. Serve warm, enjoy!

Roasted New Potatoes

Servings: 4

Cooking Time: 25 Minutes

Ingredients:

- ➢ 2 Pound small new potatoes
- ➢ 3 Tablespoon butter, melted
- ➢ 2 Tablespoon olive oil
- ➢ 2 Tablespoon whole mustard seeds
- ➢ salt and pepper
- ➢ 2 Tablespoon freshly minced chives
- ➢ 2 Tablespoon freshly minced parsley

Directions:

1. Place potatoes in a colander and rinse with cold water. Dry on paper towels and transfer to a rimmed baking sheet large enough to hold them in a single layer.

2. Drizzle the potatoes with butter and olive oil, then sprinkle them with the mustard seeds. Season with salt and pepper.

3. Supply your smoker with wood pellets and follow the start-up procedure. Preheat the grill, with the lid closed, to 400° F.

4. Place the baking sheet with the potatoes on the grill grate. Roast for about 25 minutes shaking the pan once or twice, until potatoes are tender and the skins are slightly wrinkled. Grill: 400 °F

5. Transfer potatoes to a bowl or platter. Top with fresh chives and parsley. Enjoy!

POULTRY RECIPES

Delicious Smoked Turketta

Servings: 6

Cooking Time: 180 Minutes

Ingredients:

➢ 1 Shady Brook Farms® Turketta

Directions:

1. Supply your smoker with wood pellets and follow the start-up procedure. Preheat the grill, with the lid closed, to 250° F. If using a gas or charcoal grill, set it up for low, indirect heat.

2. Place the Turketta directly on the grill grate and smoke for 2½ to 3 hours, or until an internal temperature of 165°F is reached.

Smoked Ditch Chicken

Servings: 2

Cooking Time: 60 Minutes

Ingredients:

- 3 pheasant breasts or quarters
- Blackened Saskatchewan Rub
- 3 Tablespoon Smoky Okie's Rooster Booster Poultry Seasoning
- 1 white onion
- 1 red bell pepper
- 4 Tablespoon olive oil
- salt and pepper
- 1 Box Uncle Ben's Ready Rice Pilaf

Directions:

1. Supply your smoker with wood pellets and follow the start-up procedure. Preheat the grill, with the lid closed, to 275° F.

2. Clean and rinse pheasant breasts and thighs; place in a large resealable bag.

3. Add a liberal amount of Traeger Blackened Saskatchewan Rub and Rooster Booster. Shake vigorously and set aside.

4. Slice the onions into thin sections. Quarter the peppers, removing the core.

5. Brush onions and peppers lightly with olive oil and lightly apply salt and pepper.

6. Place the vegetables on tin foil on one side of the grill. Give the vegetables an ample head start on the pheasant (at least an hour), as pheasant is lean and will cook quickly.

7. After allowing the vegetables to smoke for at least an hour, place the pheasant on the grill, keeping the grill at 275°F. Cook for 30 to 45 minutes. Remove the pheasant and vegetables from the grill and serve over a bed of rice pilaf. Enjoy! Grill: 275 °F

Grilled Honey Chicken Kabobs

Servings: 4

Cooking Time: 14 Minutes

Ingredients:

- ➢ 1 pound boneless skinless chicken breasts (cut into 1 inch pieces)
- ➢ 1/4 cup olive oil
- ➢ 1/3 cup soy sauce
- ➢ 1/4 cup honey
- ➢ 1 teaspoon minced garlic
- ➢ salt and pepper to taste
- ➢ 1 red bell pepper (cut into 1 inch pieces)
- ➢ 1 yellow bell pepper (cut into 1 inch pieces)
- ➢ 2 small zucchini (cut into 1 inch slices)
- ➢ 1 red onion (cut into 1 inch pieces)
- ➢ 1 tablespoon chopped parsley

Directions:

1. In a large bowl combine the olive oil, soy sauce, honey, garlic and salt and pepper, and whisk.
2. Add the chicken, bell peppers, zucchini and red onion to the bowl,tossing to thoroughly coat.
3. Cover and refrigerate for 1 to 8 hours.
4. Soak wooden skewers in cold water for at least 30 minutes. Supply your smoker with wood pellets and follow the start-up procedure. Preheat the grill, with the lid closed, to high heat.
5. Thread the chicken and vegetables onto the skewers.
6. Cook for 5-7 minutes on each side or until chicken is cooked through.
7. To serve, sprinkle with parsley. Enjoy!

Nashville Spiced Smoked Chicken

Servings: 6

Cooking Time: 40 Minutes

Ingredients:

- 6 drumsticks
- 1 quart Butter Milk
- 1 tbsp Louisiana Hot Sauce
- 1 tbsp Ground Cumin
- 1/2 tbsp Chili powder
- 1 tbsp Onion Powder
- 1 tbsp Garlic Powder
- 1/2 tbsp White Pepper
- 1 tbsp Red Cayenne Pepper
- 1 tbsp Black Pepper
- 2 tbsp Brown Sugar

Directions:

1. Soak wings overnight in marinade.
2. Remove chicken from marinade.Dry off chicken and wash off buttermilk.
3. Drizzle chicken with olive oil.
4. Apply dry rub to drumsticks by rubbing thoroughly.
5. Let drumsticks rest in dry rub for at least 30 minutes.
6. Supply your smoker with wood pellets and follow the start-up procedure. Preheat the grill, with the lid closed, to 325° F, using Apple Wood Pellets.
7. Cook chicken on 325 degrees for 30-40 minutes or until internal temperature reach 160 degrees F.
8. Let chicken rest for 10 minutes before serving.

Spiced Cornish Hens With Cilantro Chutney

Servings: 2   Cooking Time: 60 Minutes

Ingredients:

- 2 Cornish game hens, each about 1 to 1¼lb (450 to 565g), thawed if frozen
- 1 small white onion, peeled and halved
- 4 slices of fresh ginger
- 4 garlic cloves, peeled
- 3 tbsp vegetable oil
- 2 tsp garam masala
- for the brine
- ½ gallon (1.9 liters) distilled water
- ½ cup kosher salt
- for the chutney
- 1 bunch of cilantro, washed and roughly chopped
- 4 scallions, trimmed and roughly chopped
- 2 garlic cloves, peeled and roughly chopped
- 2 small green chili peppers, deseeded and minced
- 1-inch (2.5cm) piece of fresh ginger, peeled and minced
- 1 tbsp dry-roasted peanuts
- 1 tsp coarse salt
- 1 tsp ground cumin
- ½ tsp ground coriander
- 3 tbsp freshly squeezed lemon juice
- ¼ cup extra virgin olive oil

Directions:

1. In a stockpot on the stovetop over medium-high heat, make the brine by bringing the water and salt to a boil. Stir until the salt dissolves. Remove the pot from the stovetop and let the brine cool to room temperature. Cover and refrigerate until cool.

2. Submerge the hens in the brine. If they float, place a resealable bag of ice on top. Cover and refrigerate for 4 hours or as long as 8 hours.

3. Supply your smoker with wood pellets and follow the start-up procedure. Preheat the grill, with the lid closed, to 350° F.

4. In a blender, make the chutney by combining all the ingredients except the olive oil. Blend until the ingredients begin to move, adding 1 tablespoon of water if they need help. When a paste has formed, add the olive oil in a thin stream until the chutney is smooth. If it seems too thick, add a small bit of water. If it's too thin, add a little more oil. Store in a covered container in the refrigerator until ready to use.

5. Remove the hens from the brine. Rinse inside and out under cold running water and pat dry with paper towels. Place half an onion, 2 slices of ginger, and 2 garlic cloves in the cavity of each hen. Tie the legs together with butcher's twine.

6. In a small bowl, combine the vegetable oil and garam masala. Rub the mixture thinly and evenly on the outside of the hens.

7. Place the hens on the grate and roast until they're nicely browned and the internal temperature in the thickest part of a thigh reaches 165°F (74°C), about 1 hour.

8. Transfer the hens to a platter. Serve with the chutney.

Lemon Chicken Breast

Servings: 6   Cooking Time: 15 Minutes

Ingredients:

- ➢ 1 Clove garlic, coarsely chopped
- ➢ 2 Teaspoon honey
- ➢ 2 Teaspoon kosher salt
- ➢ 1 Teaspoon freshly ground black pepper
- ➢ 2 Sprig fresh thyme leaves
- ➢ 1 lemon, zest and juice
- ➢ 1/2 Cup high-quality olive oil or vegetable oil
- ➢ 6 (6 oz) boneless, skinless chicken breasts
- ➢ 1 lemon, cut into wedges, for serving

Directions:

1. To make the marinade, add the garlic, honey, salt, pepper, thyme, lemon juice and zest to a small mixing bowl. Whisk until the salt crystals and honey dissolve. Slowly whisk in the olive oil.

2. Place the chicken breast in a large resealable plastic bag and pour the marinade over them, massaging the bag to distribute the marinade evenly.

3. Refrigerate for 4 hours.

4. Supply your smoker with wood pellets and follow the start-up procedure. Preheat the grill, with the lid closed, to 400° F.

5. Drain the chicken breasts and discard the marinade.

6. Arrange the chicken breasts directly on the grill grate and cook until the internal temperature reaches 165°F. Grill: 400 °F Probe: 165 °F

7. If desired, grill the reserved lemon wedges alongside the chicken, cut sides down, for 15 minutes.

8. Serve the chicken on a platter or plates with the lemon wedges.

Savory Jerk Chicken Wings

Servings: 4

Cooking Time: 20 Minutes

Ingredients:

- 1 Tsp Allspice, Ground
- 3 Lbs Chicken Wings, Split
- 1/2 Tsp Cinnamon, Ground
- 4 Garlic Cloves, Smashed
- 2 Tsp Ginger, Grated
- 1 Habanero Pepper, Chopped
- 2 Tbsp Honey
- 2 Tbsp Lemon Juice
- 1/3 Cup Lime Juice
- 1/2 Tsp Nutmeg, Ground
- 1/2 Cup Olive Oil
- 1/4 Cup Poblano Pepper, Chopped
- 1 Tbsp Tamari
- 2 Tsp Thyme, Dried
- 1/2 Cup Yellow Onion, Chopped

Directions:

1. Add chicken to a large resealable plastic bag.

2. In the bowl of a food processor, add the garlic, onion, ginger, peppers, tamari, honey, lime juice, lemon juice, thyme, allspice, cinnamon, nutmeg, and oil. Process on low for 1 minute, then transfer marinade to the bag. Seal the bag and place in the refrigerator for at least 2 hours, up to overnight.

3. Supply your smoker with wood pellets and follow the start-up procedure. Preheat the grill, with the lid open, to 425° F. If using a gas or charcoal grill, set it up for medium-high heat.

4. Remove wings from the marinade, and discard remaining marinade. Place wings on the grill and cook for 15 to 20 minutes, flipping every 5 minutes, until an internal temperature of 165 F is reached.

5. Remove wings from the grill and serve warm.

Smoked Thanksgiving Turkey

Servings: 6 - 8

Cooking Time: 300 Minutes

Ingredients:

➢ 1 Turkey Brining Kits

➢ 12 – 14 Lbs Turkey

➢ 1 Gallon Water, Cold

➢ 4 Cups + 1 Gallon Water, Warm

Directions:

1. Start by defrosting the turkey overnight in the refrigerator.

2. Once turkey has been defrosted begin to make the brine by adding 4 cups of water and the brine mixture to a large stockpot.

3. Bring the mixture to a boil and add 1 gallon of cold water.

4. Place the turkey in the brine bag and pour the brine mixture over the turkey and refrigerate 1 hour per pound.

5. Once turkey has been brined rinse the turkey with cold water and set on a pan.

6. Using the seasoning in the brine box, season the turkey. Once turkey has been seasoned, supply your smoker with wood pellets and follow the start-up procedure. Preheat the grill, with the lid closed, to 275° F.

7. Place your turkey in the smoker and place the temperature probe in the deepest part of the breast. Cook at 275 until the breast and thigh meat internal temperature has reached 165°F to 170°F.

8. Remove the turkey from the smoker, let cool, and cut the turkey into your desired pieces. Enjoy!

Grilled Whole Chicken Stuffed Sausage And Apple

Servings: 4

Cooking Time: 90 Minutes

Ingredients:

- ¼ Tbsp Black Pepper
- 1 Tbsp Butter, Unsalted
- 1 Celery, Stalk
- ¾ Cup Chicken Broth
- ¼ Tbsp Dried Sage
- 1 ½ Cup Dry Stuffing, Unseasoned
- 1 Granny Smith Apple, Chopped
- 8 Oz. Italian Sausage, Casings Removed
- ½ Tbsp Olive Oil
- 3 Tbsp Tennessee Apple Butter Rub
- ¼ Tbsp Salt
- ¼ White Onion, Chopped
- ½ White Onion, Sliced
- 3-4 Lb. Whole Chicken

Directions:

1. Supply your smoker with wood pellets and follow the start-up procedure. Preheat the grill, with the lid open, to 400° F. If using a gas or charcoal grill, set it up for medium-high heat.

2. Meanwhile, rinse chicken thoroughly and dry with paper towel. Place sliced onion in cast iron pan and set chicken on top. Place stuffing inside chicken cavity. Sprinkle Tennessee Apple Butter seasoning all over chicken and rub into skin. Tuck wings under.

3. Transfer to pellet grill and cook for 45 minutes. Add 1 cup chicken stock to pan, rotate and cook an additional 30 minutes. Remove from grill when internal temperature reaches 165° F and there is even browning. Allow chicken to rest for 15 minutes, then carve and serve.

Easy Bbq Chicken Wings

Servings: 4

Cooking Time: 40 Minutes

Ingredients:

- 1 Pack Chicken Wings
- Extra Virgin Olive Oil
- Champion Chicken Seasoning

Directions:

1. Supply your smoker with wood pellets and follow the start-up procedure. Preheat the grill, with the lid closed, to 350° F.

2. Blot the defrosted chicken wings dry with paper towels.

3. Brush oil onto each side of the wings and sprinkle with seasoning.

4. Grill at 350° for 40 minutes or until wings are crispy. Flip halfway through. Serve hot.

Asian Chicken Sliders

| Servings: 4 | Cooking Time: 10 Minutes |

Ingredients:

- 1½lb (680g) ground chicken, preferably a mix of breast and thigh meat
- 1 large egg, beaten
- ½ cup panko breadcrumbs or crushed chicharróns
- 2 scallions, trimmed, white and green parts finely minced
- 2 garlic cloves, peeled and finely minced
- ¼ cup loosely packed minced cilantro leaves
- 2 tbsp sambal oelek
- 1 tbsp light soy sauce
- 2 tsp peeled and minced fresh ginger
- 1 tsp coarse salt
- 1 tsp freshly ground black pepper
- vegetable oil
- for serving
- 8 slider buns
- reduced-fat mayo
- fresh baby arugula or spinach leaves
- pickled onions (optional)

Directions:

1. Supply your smoker with wood pellets and follow the start-up procedure. Preheat the grill, with the lid closed, to 450° F.

2. In a large bowl, combine all the ingredients except the vegetable oil. Wet your hands with cold water. Knead the mixture until it's somewhat sticky and the ingredients are incorporated. Form the mixture into 8 equal-sized patties. Lightly oil the patties on both sides with the oil.

3. Place the patties on the grate and grill until the internal temperature reaches 165°F (74°C), about 4 to 5 minutes per side.

4. Transfer each patty to the bottom half of each bun. Top with a dollop of mayo, a few arugula or spinach leaves, and drained pickled onions (if using). Top each slider with the top half of the bun. Run a knotted bamboo skewer through the top of each slider before serving.

Lollipop Drumsticks

| Servings: 4-6 | Cooking Time: 75 Minutes |

Ingredients:

- ➤ 1 Cup Barbecue Sauce
- ➤ 10 Tablespoons Butter, Salted
- ➤ 12 Chicken Drumsticks
- ➤ 1 Cup Hot Sauce
- ➤ Champion Chicken Seasoning
- ➤ Blue Cheese Or Ranch Dressing

Directions:

1. Supply your smoker with wood pellets and follow the start-up procedure. Preheat the grill, with the lid open, to 300° F.

2. Rinse chicken and pat dry with a paper towel.

3. Chop the very top of the drumstick on the larger, meaty side so the lollipops sit flatly. On the small end of the drumstick, about an inch above the knuckle, use a sharp knife or kitchen shears to cut the skin and tendons all the way down to the bone and pull the skin and cartilage off the knuckle.

4. Remove the tiny, sharp bone that sits right against the exposed chicken leg. Then, push all the meat and skin down to form the lollipop ball. Use your knife or shears to remove any excess tendons.

5. Season each lollipop generously with Champion Chicken seasoning and place in the aluminum pan with the flat side done and bones standing straight up. Then, cut 10 tablespoons of butter into cubes of 1 tablespoon each and place evenly throughout the rows of lollipops.

6. Cook lollipop drumsticks on your   at 300°F for 1 hour; checking back every 20 minutes to baste the meat with the melted butter on the bottom of the pan.

7. For the Sauce: add your favorite bbq sauce into one aluminum loaf pan. Then, add 1 cup of hot sauce and 10 tablespoons of butter into the other aluminum loaf pan. Place them on the grill 5 minutes before your chicken is done. Stir well once it's warm and the butter has melted.

8. After 1 hour, use a thermometer to check the internal temperature of the lollipops. They will be ready to glaze when the temperature reaches 165°F.

9. Once ready, dip 6 lollipops in the bbq sauce and 6 in the buffalo sauce making sure to hold the leg and cover the meat entirely. Then, place the lollipops on the wing rack and put back on the grill for 15 more minutes or until the sauce is set.

Lemon Cajun Chicken Carbonara

Servings: 2   Cooking Time: 20 Minutes

Ingredients:

- 2 Slices Thick-Cut Bacon
- 1 Tbsp Cajun Seasoning
- 8 Oz. Chicken Breast
- 4 Egg, Yolk
- 1 Tbsp Garlic Clove, Minced
- 1 ¼ Cup Heavy Cream
- 2 Tbsp + 1 Tbsp Divided Italian Parsley

- 1 ½ Tbsp Divided Olive Oil
- ½ Cup Grated Parmesan Cheese
- ½ Tbsp Hickory Bacon Seasoning
- ¼ Tbsp Red Chili Flakes
- 1 Tbsp Scallions
- ½ Lb. Spaghetti

Directions:

1. Supply your smoker with wood pellets and follow the start-up procedure. Preheat the grill, with the lid open, to 400° F. If using a gas or charcoal grill, set the temp to medium-high heat. In a medium bowl, combine chicken,   Hickory Bacon Seasoning, Cajun seasoning, and ½ tablespoon of olive oil. Toss to combine. Set aside or place in a bag and marinate in the refrigerator for 30 minutes to 1 hour.

2. Place tenders on preheated grill and cook for 3 minutes per side. Remove from grill and place on a cutting board to rest for 5 minutes. Slice thinly on the diagonal and set aside.

3. In a large stock pot, boil pasta per package instructions. Drain and set aside.

4. In a large skillet heat 1 tablespoon of oil over medium heat. Sauté bacon, stirring frequently, for 3 minutes or until crisp. Add garlic and cook for one minute. Lower heat to low and add in drained pasta. Using tongs, gently toss pasta to coat in oil and bacon.

5. In a mixing bowl, whisk together heavy cream, parmesan, egg yolks, and 2 tablespoons of parsley. Slowly pour over pasta, continuously stirring, as to not scramble eggs. After 2 minutes, the sauce will thicken. Add in chicken and lemon zest, and gently stir another minute. Transfer to serving dishes and garnish with additional parsley and red chili flakes.

APPETIZERS AND SNACKS

Bayou Wings With Cajun Rémoulade

Servings: 8   Cooking Time: 40 Minutes

Ingredients:

- 16 large whole chicken wings or 32 drumettes and flats, about 3lb (1.4kg) total
- for the rub
- 1 tbsp kosher salt
- 1 tsp freshly ground black pepper
- 1 tsp paprika
- ½ tsp ground cayenne, plus more
- ½ tsp garlic powder
- ½ tsp celery salt
- ½ tsp dried thyme
- 2 tbsp vegetable oil
- for the rémoulade
- 1¼ cups reduced-fat mayo
- ¼ cup Creole-style or whole grain mustard
- 2 tbsp horseradish
- 2 tbsp pickle relish
- 1 tbsp freshly squeezed lemon juice
- 1 tsp paprika, plus more
- 1 tsp hot sauce, plus more
- 1 tsp Worcestershire sauce
- coarse salt
- for serving
- lemon wedges
- pickled okra (optional)

Directions:

1. Supply your smoker with wood pellets and follow the start-up procedure. Preheat the grill, with the lid closed, to 350° F.

2. If using whole wings, cut through the two joints, separating them into drumettes, flats, and wing tips. (Discard the wing tips or save them for chicken stock.) Alternatively, leave the wings whole. Place the chicken in a resealable plastic bag.

3. In a small bowl, make the rub by combining the ingredients. Mix well. Pour the rub over the wings and toss them to thoroughly coat. Refrigerate for 2 hours.

4. In a small bowl, make the Cajun rémoulade by whisking together the mayo, mustard, horseradish, pickle relish, lemon juice, paprika, hot sauce, and Worcestershire. Season with salt to taste. The mixture should be highly seasoned. Transfer to a serving bowl and lightly dust with paprika. Cover and refrigerate until ready to serve.

5. Remove the wings from the refrigerator and allow the excess marinade to drip off. Place the wings on the grate at an angle to the bars. Grill for 20 minutes and then turn. (They'll brown more evenly but will also have less of a tendency to stick.) Continue to cook until the wings are nicely browned and the meat is no longer pink at the bone, about 20 minutes more.

6. Remove the wings from the grill and pile them on a platter. Serve with the Cajun rémoulade, lemon wedges, and pickled okra (if using).

Chuckwagon Beef Jerky

Ingredients:

- 2½lb (1.2kg) boneless top or bottom round steak, sirloin tip, flank steak, or venison
- 1 cup sugar-free dark-colored soda
- 1 cup cold brewed coffee
- ½ cup light soy sauce
- ¼ cup Worcestershire sauce
- 2 tbsp whiskey (optional)
- 2 tsp chili powder
- 1½ tsp garlic salt
- 1 tsp onion powder
- 1 tsp pink curing salt

Directions:

1. Slice the meat into ¼-inch-thick (.5cm) strips, trimming off any visible fat or gristle. (Slice against the grain for more tender jerky and with the grain for chewier jerky.) Place the meat in a large resealable plastic bag.

2. In a small bowl, whisk together the soda, coffee, soy sauce, Worcestershire sauce, whiskey (if using), chili powder, garlic salt, onion powder, and curing salt (if using). Whisk until the salt dissolves. Pour the mixture over the meat and reseal the bag. Refrigerate for 24 to 48 hours, turning the bag several times to redistribute the brine.

3. Supply your smoker with wood pellets and follow the start-up procedure. Preheat the grill, with the lid closed, to 150° F.

4. Drain the meat and discard the brine. Place the strips of meat in a single layer on paper towels and blot any excess moisture.

5. Place the meat in a single layer on the grate and smoke for 4 to 5 hours, turning once or twice. (If you're aware of hot spots on your grate, rotate the strips so they smoke evenly.) To test for doneness, bend one or two pieces in the middle. They should be dry but still somewhat pliant. Or simply eat a piece to see if it's done to your liking.

6. For the best texture, when you remove the meat from the grill, place the still-warm jerky in a resealable plastic bag and let rest for 30 minutes. (You might see condensation form on the inside of the bag, but the moisture will be reabsorbed by the meat.) Or let the meat cool completely and then store in a resealable plastic bag or covered container. The jerky will last a few days at room temperature but will last longer (up to 2 weeks) if refrigerated.

Simple Cream Cheese Sausage Balls

Servings: 5

Cooking Time: 30 Minutes

Ingredients:

- 1 pound ground hot sausage, uncooked
- 8 ounces cream cheese, softened
- 1 package mini filo dough shells

Directions:

1. Supply your smoker with wood pellets and follow the start-up procedure. Preheat, with the lid closed, to 350°F.
2. In a large bowl, using your hands, thoroughly mix together the sausage and cream cheese until well blended.
3. Place the filo dough shells on a rimmed perforated pizza pan or into a mini muffin tin.
4. Roll the sausage and cheese mixture into 1-inch balls and place into the filo shells.
5. Place the pizza pan or mini muffin tin on the grill, close the lid, and smoke the sausage balls for 30 minutes, or until cooked through and the sausage is no longer pink.
6. Plate and serve warm.

Pigs In A Blanket

Servings: 4-6

Cooking Time: 15 Minutes

Ingredients:

- 2 Tablespoon Poppy Seeds
- 1 Tablespoon Dried Minced Onion
- 2 Teaspoon garlic, minced
- 2 Tablespoon Sesame Seeds
- 1 Teaspoon salt
- 8 Ounce Original Crescent Dough
- 1/4 Cup Dijon mustard
- 1 Large egg, beaten

Directions:

1. When ready to cook, start your smoker at 350 degrees F, and preheat with lid closed, 10 to 15 minutes.

2. Mix together poppy seeds, dried minced onion, dried minced garlic, salt and sesame seeds. Set aside.

3. Cut each triangle of crescent roll dough into thirds lengthwise, making 3 small strips from each roll.

4. Brush the dough strips lightly with Dijon mustard. Put the mini hot dogs on 1 end of the dough and roll up.

5. Arrange them, seam side down, on a greased baking pan. Brush with egg wash and sprinkle with seasoning mixture.

6. Bake in smoker until golden brown, about 12 to 15 minutes.

7. Serve with mustard or dipping sauce of your choice. Enjoy!

Sriracha & Maple Cashews

Servings: 10

Cooking Time: 60 Minutes

Ingredients:

- 2 tbsp unsalted butter
- 3 tbsp pure maple syrup
- 1 tbsp sriracha
- 1 tsp coarse salt (use only if nuts are unsalted)
- 2½ cups unsalted cashews

Directions:

1. Supply your smoker with wood pellets and follow the start-up procedure. Preheat the grill, with the lid closed, to 250° F.

2. In a small saucepan on the stovetop over low heat, melt the butter. Add the maple syrup, sriracha, and salt (if using). Stir until combined. Add the nuts and stir gently to coat thoroughly.

3. Spread the nuts in a single layer in an aluminum foil roasting pan coated with cooking spray. Place the pan on the grate and smoke the nuts until they're lightly toasted, about 1 hour, stirring once or twice.

4. Remove the pan from the grill and let the nuts cool for 15 minutes. They'll be sticky at first but will crisp up. Break them up with your fingers and store at room temperature in an airtight container, such as a lidded glass jar.

Smoked Turkey Sandwich

Servings: 1

Cooking Time: 15 Minutes

Ingredients:

- ➢ 2 slices sourdough bread
- ➢ 2 tablespoons butter, at room temperature
- ➢ 2 (1-ounce) slices Swiss cheese
- ➢ 4 ounces leftover Smoked Turkey
- ➢ 1 teaspoon garlic salt

Directions:

1. Supply your smoker with wood pellets and follow the start-up procedure. Preheat the grill, with the lid closed, to 375°F.

2. Coat one side of each bread slice with 1 tablespoon of butter and sprinkle the buttered sides with garlic salt.

3. Place 1 slice of cheese on each unbuttered side of the bread, and then put the turkey on the cheese.

4. Close the sandwich, buttered sides out, and place it directly on the grill grate. Cook for 5 minutes. Flip the sandwich and cook for 5 minutes more. Remove the sandwich from the grill, cut it in half, and serve.

Pulled Pork Loaded Nachos

Servings: 4

Cooking Time: 10 Minutes

Ingredients:

- 2 cups leftover smoked pulled pork
- 1 small sweet onion, diced
- 1 medium tomato, diced
- 1 jalapeño pepper, seeded and diced
- 1 garlic clove, minced
- 1 teaspoon salt
- 1 teaspoon freshly ground black pepper
- 1 bag tortilla chips
- 1 cup shredded Cheddar cheese
- ½ cup The Ultimate BBQ Sauce, divided
- ½ cup shredded jalapeño Monterey Jack cheese
- Juice of ½ lime
- 1 avocado, halved, pitted, and sliced
- 2 tablespoons sour cream
- 1 tablespoon chopped fresh cilantro

Directions:

1. Supply your smoker with wood pellets and follow the start-up procedure. Preheat, with the lid closed, to 375°F.

2. Heat the pulled pork in the microwave.

3. In a medium bowl, combine the onion, tomato, jalapeño, garlic, salt, and pepper, and set aside.

4. Arrange half of the tortilla chips in a large cast iron skillet. Spread half of the warmed pork on top and cover with the Cheddar cheese. Top with half of the onion-jalapeño mixture, then drizzle with ¼ cup of barbecue sauce.

5. Layer on the remaining tortilla chips, then the remaining pork and the Monterey Jack cheese. Top with the remaining onion-jalapeño mixture and drizzle with the remaining ¼ cup of barbecue sauce.

6. Place the skillet on the grill, close the lid, and smoke for about 10 minutes, or until the cheese is melted and bubbly. (Watch to make sure your chips don't burn!)

7. Squeeze the lime juice over the nachos, top with the avocado slices and sour cream, and garnish with the cilantro before serving hot.

Jalapeño Poppers With Chipotle Sour Cream

Servings: 8   Cooking Time: 45 Minutes

Ingredients:

- 3 strips of thin-sliced bacon
- 12 large jalapeños, red, green, or a mix
- 8oz (225g) light cream cheese, at room temperature
- 1 cup shredded pepper Jack, Monterey Jack, or Cheddar cheese
- 1 tsp chili powder
- ½ tsp garlic salt
- smoked paprika
- for the sour cream
- 1¼ cups light sour cream
- juice of ½ lime
- ½ to 1 canned chipotle peppers in adobo sauce, finely minced, plus 1 tsp of sauce, plus more
- 1 tbsp minced fresh cilantro leaves
- ½ tsp coarse salt, plus more

Directions:

1. Supply your smoker with wood pellets and follow the start-up procedure. Preheat the grill, with the lid closed, to 375° F.

2. Line a rimmed sheet pan with aluminum foil and place a wire rack on top. Place the bacon in a single layer on the wire rack. Place the pan on the grate and grill until the bacon is crisp and golden brown, about 20 minutes. Transfer the bacon to paper towels to cool and then crumble. Set aside.

3. In a small bowl, make the chipotle sour cream by whisking together the ingredients. Add more salt, chipotle peppers, or adobe sauce to taste. Cover and refrigerate.

4. Slice the jalapeños lengthwise through their stems. Scrape out the veins and seeds with the edge of a small metal spoon.

5. In a small bowl, beat together the cream cheese, shredded cheese, chili powder, and garlic salt. Stir in the crumbled bacon. Mound the cream cheese mixture in the jalapeño halves. Line another rimmed sheet pan with aluminum foil and place a wire rack on top. Place the jalapeños filled side up in a single layer on the wire rack.

6. Place the sheet pan on the grate and roast the jalapeños until the filling has melted and the peppers have softened, about 20 to 25 minutes. (They should no longer look bright in color.) Remove the pan from the grill and let the peppers rest for 5 minutes.

7. Transfer the poppers to a platter and lightly dust with paprika. Serve with the chipotle sour cream.

Grilled Guacamole

Servings: 6

Cooking Time: 30 Minutes

Ingredients:

- 3 large avocados, halved and pitted
- 1 lime, halved
- ½ jalapeño, deseeded and deveined
- ½ small white or red onion, peeled
- 2 garlic cloves, peeled and skewered on a toothpick
- 1 tsp coarse salt, plus more
- 1½ tbsp reduced-fat mayo
- 2 tbsp chopped fresh cilantro
- 2 tbsp crumbled queso fresco (optional)
- tortilla chips

Directions:

1. Supply your smoker with wood pellets and follow the start-up procedure. Preheat the grill, with the lid closed, to 225° F.

2. Place the avocados, lime, jalapeño, and onion cut sides down on the grate. Use the toothpicks to balance the garlic cloves between the bars. Smoke for 30 minutes. (You want the vegetables to retain most of their rawness.)

3. Transfer everything to a cutting board. Remove the garlic cloves from the toothpick and roughly chop. Sprinkle with the salt and continue to mince the garlic until it begins to form a paste. Scrape the garlic and salt into a large bowl.

4. Scoop the avocado flesh from the peels into the bowl. Squeeze the juice of ½ lime over the avocado. Mash the avocados but leave them somewhat chunky. Finely dice the jalapeño. Dice 2 tablespoons of onion. (Reserve the remaining onion for another use.) Add the jalapeño, onion, mayo, and cilantro to the bowl. Stir gently to combine. Taste for seasoning, adding more salt, lime juice, and jalapeño as desired.

5. Transfer the guacamole to a serving bowl. Top with the queso fresco (if using). Serve with tortilla chips.

Bacon Pork Pinwheels (kansas Lollipops)

Servings: 4-6

Cooking Time: 20 Minutes

Ingredients:

- 1 Whole Pork Loin, boneless
- To Taste salt and pepper
- To Taste Greek Seasoning
- 4 Slices bacon
- To Taste The Ultimate BBQ Sauce

Directions:

1. When ready to cook, start the smoker and set temperature to 500F. Preheat, lid closed, for 10 to 15 minutes.

2. Trim pork loin of any unwanted silver skin or fat. Using a sharp knife, cut pork loin length wise, into 4 long strips.

3. Lay pork flat, then season with salt, pepper and Cavender's Greek Seasoning.

4. Flip the pork strips over and layer bacon on unseasoned side. Begin tightly rolling the pork strips, with bacon being rolled up on the inside.

5. Secure a skewer all the way through each pork roll to secure it in place. Set the pork rolls down on grill and cook for 15 minutes.

6. Brush BBQ Sauce over the pork. Turn each skewer over, then coat the other side. Let pork cook for another 5-10 minutes, depending on thickness of your pork. Enjoy!

Citrus-infused Marinated Olives

Servings: 6

Cooking Time: 30 Minutes

Ingredients:

➢ 1½ cups mixed brined olives, with pits

➢ ½ cup extra virgin olive oil

➢ 1 tbsp freshly squeezed lemon juice

➢ 1 garlic clove, peeled and thinly sliced

➢ 1 tsp smoked Spanish paprika

➢ 2 sprigs of fresh rosemary

➢ 2 sprigs of fresh thyme

➢ 2 bay leaves, fresh or dried

➢ 1 small dried red chili pepper, deseeded and flesh crumbled, or ¼ tsp crushed red pepper flakes

➢ 3 strips of orange zest

➢ 3 strips of lemon zest

Directions:

1. Supply your smoker with wood pellets and follow the start-up procedure. Preheat the grill, with the lid closed, to 180° F.

2. Drain the olives, reserving 1 tablespoon of brine. Spread the olives in a single layer in an aluminum foil roasting pan. Place the pan on the grate and cook the olives for 30 minutes, stirring the olives or shaking the pan once or twice.

3. In a small saucepan on the stovetop over low heat, warm the olive oil. Whisk in the lemon juice and the reserved 1 tablespoon of brine. Stir in the garlic and paprika. Add the rosemary, thyme, bay leaves, chili pepper, and orange and lemon zests. Warm over low heat for 10 minutes. Remove the saucepan from the heat.

4. Transfer the olives and olive oil mixture to a pint jar. Tuck the aromatics around the sides of the jar. Let cool and then cover and refrigerate for up to 5 days. Let the olives come to room temperature before serving.

Roasted Red Pepper Dip

Servings: 8

Cooking Time: 45 Minutes

Ingredients:

- 4 red bell peppers, halved, destemmed, and deseeded
- 1 cup English walnuts, divided
- 1 small white onion, peeled and coarsely chopped
- 2 garlic cloves, peeled and smashed with a chef's knife
- ¼ cup extra virgin olive oil, plus more
- 1 tbsp balsamic vinegar or balsamic glaze
- 1 tsp honey (eliminate if using balsamic glaze)
- 1 tsp coarse salt, plus more
- 1 tsp ground cumin
- 1 tsp smoked paprika
- ½ to 1 tsp Aleppo red pepper flakes, plus more
- ¼ cup fresh white breadcrumbs (optional)
- distilled water (optional)
- assorted crudités or wedges of pita bread

Directions:

1. Supply your smoker with wood pellets and follow the start-up procedure. Preheat the grill, with the lid closed, to 400° F.

2. Place the peppers skin side down on the grate and grill until the skins blister and the flesh softens, about 30 minutes. Transfer the peppers to a bowl and cover with plastic wrap. Let cool to room temperature. Remove the skins with a paring knife or your fingers. Coarsely chop or tear the peppers.

3. Place ¾ cup of walnuts in an aluminum foil roasting pan. Place the pan on the grate and toast for 10 to 15 minutes, stirring twice. Remove the pan from the grill and let the walnuts cool.

4. Place the peppers, onion, garlic, and walnuts in a food processor fitted with the chopping blade. Pulse several times. Add the olive oil, balsamic vinegar, honey, salt, cumin, paprika, and red pepper flakes. Process until the mixture is fairly smooth. Taste for seasoning, adding more salt or red pepper flakes (if desired). (If the mixture is too loose, add breadcrumbs until the texture is to your liking. If it's too thick, add olive oil or water 1 tablespoon at a time.)

5. Transfer the dip to a serving bowl. Use the back of a spoon to make a shallow depression in the center. Top with the remaining ¼ cup of walnuts and drizzle olive oil in the depression. Serve with crudités or pita bread.

Deviled Eggs With Smoked Paprika

Servings: 6   Cooking Time: 30 Minutes

Ingredients:

- 6 large eggs
- 3 tbsp reduced-fat mayo, plus more
- 1 tsp Dijon or yellow mustard
- ½ tsp Spanish smoked paprika or regular paprika, plus more
- dash of hot sauce
- coarse salt
- freshly ground black pepper
- for garnishing
- small sprigs of fresh parsley, dill, tarragon, or cilantro
- chopped chives
- minced scallions
- Mustard Caviar
- sliced green or black olives
- celery leaves
- sliced radishes
- diced bell peppers
- sliced cherry tomatoes
- fresh or pickled jalapeños
- sliced or diced pickles
- slivers of sun-dried tomatoes
- bacon crumbles
- smoked salmon
- Hawaiian black salt
- Caviar

Directions:

1. Supply your smoker with wood pellets and follow the start-up procedure. Preheat the grill, with the lid closed, to 180° F.

2. On the stovetop over medium-high heat, bring a saucepan of water to a boil. (Make sure there's enough water in the saucepan to cover the eggs by 1 inch [5cm].) Use a slotted spoon to gently lower the eggs into the water. Lower the heat to maintain a simmer. Set a timer for 13 minutes.

3. Prepare an ice bath by combining ice and cold water in a large bowl. Carefully transfer the eggs to the ice bath when the timer goes off.

4. When the eggs are cool enough to handle, gently tap them all over to crack the shell. Carefully peel the eggs. Rinse under cold running water to remove any clinging bits of shell, but don't dry the eggs. (A damp surface will help the smoke adhere to the egg whites.)

5. Place the eggs on the grate and smoke until the eggs take on a light brown patina from the smoke, about 25 minutes. Transfer the eggs to a cutting board, handling them as little as possible.

6. Slice each egg in half lengthwise with a sharp knife. Wipe any yolk off the blade before slicing the next egg. Gently remove the yolks and place them in a food processor. Pulse to break up the yolks. Add the mayo, mustard, paprika, and hot sauce. Season with salt and pepper to taste. Pulse until the filling is smooth. Add additional mayo 1 teaspoon at a time if the mixture is a little dry. (It shouldn't be too loose either.)

7. Spoon the filling into each egg half or pipe it in using a small resealable plastic bag. You can also use a pastry bag fitted with a fluted tip.

8. Place the eggs on a platter and lightly dust with paprika. Accompany with one or more of the suggested garnishes.

BEEF LAMB AND GAME RECIPES

Reverse Sear Tomahawk Chop

Servings: 4

Cooking Time: 60 Minutes

Ingredients:

- 2 Tbsp Coarsely Ground Black Peppercorns
- 1 Melted Stick Butter, Salted
- 2 Tablespoons Chophouse Steak Seasoning
- 2 Tbsp Sea Salt
- 2 Tsp Sprigs Fresh Thyme, Minced
- 2 Steaks, Tomahawk

Directions:

1. In a small mixing bowl, add the black peppercorns, sea salt, Chophouse Seasoning, and fresh thyme. Mix together and reserve half the seasoning.

2. Place your Tomahawk Steaks onto a sheet pan covered with butcher paper, foil, or parchment paper. Generously season the steaks with the seasoning mixture and rub it into the steaks. Let steaks sit for 1-2 hours if you would like the seasoning to penetrate the meat.

3. Supply your smoker with wood pellets and follow the start-up procedure. Preheat the grill, with the lid closed, to 225° F. If you're using a gas or charcoal grill, set it up for low, indirect heat. Insert a temperature probe into the thickest part of one of the tomahawk chops and place them in the center of the grill. If you have 2 temperature probes insert another into the other steak. Grill until the internal temperature of the steaks reaches 110°F, about 30-40 minutes.

4. Once the steaks reach their internal temperature, remove them from the grill and set aside. Increase the grill temperature to 450-500°F. While the grill is heating up melt one stick of butter and add the reserved seasoning to the melted butter. Mix together and brush the steaks with the butter making sure to evenly coat both sides of the steaks.

5. Place the steaks back on the grill over an open flame and sear for 3-5 min per side to reach 130°F-140°F. Remove the steaks from the grill, let them rest for 5 minutes and slice and serve immediately.

Cheddar Bacon Beef Burgers

Servings: 12

Cooking Time: 30 Minutes

Ingredients:

- Bacon Cheddar Burger Seasoning
- 3/4 Cup Bacon, Chopped
- 3 Lbs Beef, Ground
- 1 Jalapeno, Chopped
- Pepper
- 1/2 Cup Ranch Dressing
- Salt
- 1 1/2 Cups Shredded Cheddar Cheese

Directions:

1. Supply your smoker with wood pellets and follow the start-up procedure. Preheat the grill, with the lid closed, to 350° F.

2. In a small bowl, combine cheese, bacon, jalapeno and ranch dressing.

3. In a clean, large bowl, combine ground beef with enough salt and pepper to taste.

4. Form meat into patties and place on a pan. A good rule of thumb is for each patty to be about the size of the palm of your hand.

5. Using a clean glass, press into each patty, leaving the imprint of the bottom of the glass in the patty. Stuff the filling into the indent. Grill for 25 minutes or until the ground beef reaches an internal temperature of 160°F. Serve hot.

Grilled Rib Eyes With Hasselback Sweet Potatoes

Servings: 4

Cooking Time: 60 Minutes

Ingredients:

- ➢ 2 (1-1/2 to 2 lb) bone-in rib-eye steaks
- ➢ 4 sweet potatoes
- ➢ extra-virgin olive oil
- ➢ salt and pepper

Directions:

1. One hour before preparing, remove the steaks from the refrigerator to allow them to come to room temperature.

2. Supply your smoker with wood pellets and follow the start-up procedure. Preheat the grill, with the lid closed, to 400° F.

3. Place the cut potatoes on a sheet pan. Drizzle with oil and season generously with salt and pepper. Place the pan on the grill. Roast until the potatoes are browned on the outside and tender in the center, 50 to 60 minutes.

4. While the sweet potatoes are roasting, prep the steaks. Rub each steak with oil, and sprinkle salt and pepper generously over each side.

5. When the sweet potatoes are almost done, place the steaks on the grill and cook, allowing each side to sear, until the internal temperature reaches 130°F for medium-rare, 4 to 5 minutes per side. Grill: 400 °F Probe: 130 °F

6. Remove the steaks from the grill, and let rest for 10 minutes.

Slow Smoked Spiced Beef

Servings: 6

Cooking Time: 360 Minutes

Ingredients:

- 3 lb beef (roast, rump, sirloin, top, or chuck)
- 1 1/2 tsp salt
- 1 tsp pepper
- 1 tsp garlic powder
- 1 tsp smoked paprika
- 1/2 tsp onion powder
- Worcestershire sauce to rub down

Directions:

1. Supply your smoker with wood pellets and follow the start-up procedure. Preheat the grill, with the lid closed, to 215 °F.

2. Start by mixing the salt, pepper, smoked paprika, garlic, and onion powders together.

3. Give the roast a good rub down with Worcestershire sauce, and then apply the spice rub.

4. Cook it in a smoker at around 215°F for 4 to 6 hours. The roast is ready to come out when its internal temperature is between 145°F to 155 °F.

5. Before slicing, let the roast rest for 20 minutes, covered with foil.

6. To help brighten up the beef's flavors, sprinklea little salt on the slices.

7. Serve and enjoy.

Salt & Pepper Beer-braised Beef Ribs

Servings: 4

Cooking Time: 180 Minutes

Ingredients:

- 2 Rack meaty beef back ribs
- coarse kosher or sea salt
- freshly ground black pepper
- granulated garlic
- 1 1/2 Cup beer or beef stock
- 'Que BBQ Sauce

Directions:

1. If your butcher has not already done so, remove the thin papery membrane from the bone-side of the ribs by working the tip of a butter knife or a screwdriver underneath the membrane over a middle bone. Use paper towels to get a firm grip, then tear the membrane off.

2. About an hour before cooking, put the ribs in a foil pan, meat-side up, and season the ribs on both sides with the salt, pepper and granulated garlic.

3. Supply your smoker with wood pellets and follow the start-up procedure. Preheat the grill, with the lid closed, to 165° F.

4. Arrange the pan of ribs on the grill grate and smoke for 1 hour. Pour the beer into the bottom of the pan (be careful not to wash the seasonings off the ribs). Cover the pan tightly with foil. Grill: 165 ˚F

5. Increase Traeger temperature to 250°F and continue to cook the ribs until the meat is meltingly tender, about 2 to 3 hours more. Grill: 250 ˚F

6. Carefully remove the foil. Discard the braising liquid and serve the ribs with Traeger 'Que BBQ Sauce. (You can brush the sauce on the ribs and sizzle them on the grill, or you can serve the sauce on the side.) Enjoy!

Easy Breakfast Cheeseburger

Servings: 2

Cooking Time: 10 Minutes

Ingredients:

- 4 Bacon, Strip
- 6 Ounce Lean Beef, Ground
- 2 Burger Buns
- 2 Cheese, Sliced
- 2 Egg
- Pepper
- Salt

Directions:

1. Supply your smoker with wood pellets and follow the start-up procedure. Preheat the grill, with the lid closed, to 400° F.

2. Take the ground beef and divide it into two thin patties. Brush the grate with oil, then add the patties and grill them on about 2-5 minutes on each side, or until the desired doneness, pressing down to get a good sear.

3. Remove the burgers from the grill, then build your burger. Starting with the bottom bun or bread slice, add the patty, then a slice of American cheese, top with bacon, hash browns, an egg over easy, and finish with the top bun or bread slice. Now it's ready to serve!

Flavour Tri Tip Burnt Ends

Servings: 3

Cooking Time: 420 Minutes

Ingredients:

- ➢ 1/2 cup bbq sauce
- ➢ to taste, beef & brisket rub
- ➢ 1 1/2 tbsp brown sugar
- ➢ 1 1/2 tbsp butter, cubed
- ➢ 1/2 cup dr. pepper soda
- ➢ 1/2 tbsp honey
- ➢ 2 tbsp mustard
- ➢ 2 lbs tri tip steak
- ➢ 1/2 tbsp worcestershire sauce

Directions:

1. Supply your smoker with wood pellets and follow the start-up procedure. Preheat the grill, with the lid closed, to 225° F. If using a gas or charcoal grill, set it up for low, indirect heat.

2. Rub the mustard all over the tri tip, then season with Beef & Brisket rub.

3. Place the tri tip directly on the grill grates and smoke until the internal temperature reaches 165° F (about 2 1/2 hours).

4. Remove the tri tip from the grill and wrap it in butcher paper. Return the tri tip to the grill and continue to smoke until the internal temperature reaches 200° F (an additional 2 ½ to 3 hours).

5. Remove the tri tip from the grill, and rest for 30 minutes, or rest and refrigerate overnight.

6. Increase the grill temperature to 275° F.

7. Cube into ½ inch to ¾ inch pieces, then place cubed tri tip in a large cast iron skillet.

8. Stir together BBQ sauce, Dr. Pepper, honey, and worcestershire sauce in a jar or mixing bowl, then pour over the cubed tri tip. Dot with butter, then sprinkle brown sugar over the top.

9. Place skillet on the grill grate, over indirect heat. Cook for 1 ½ to 2 hours, rotating pieces halfway through cooking. Sauce will have reduced, coated and slightly char the tri tip. Remove from the grill and serve warm.

Garlic Parmesan Grilled Filet Mignon

Servings: 2

Cooking Time: 10 Minutes

Ingredients:

- ➢ 4 filet mignon steaks
- ➢ 1 Teaspoon salt
- ➢ 1 Teaspoon black pepper
- ➢ 1 Teaspoon garlic salt
- ➢ 1 Cup Parmesan cheese
- ➢ 4 garlic
- ➢ 1 Tablespoon Dijon mustard

Directions:

1. Supply your smoker with wood pellets and follow the start-up procedure. Preheat the grill, with the lid closed, to High heat.

2. While the grill is heating up, season the filets with salt, pepper, and garlic salt. Also mince your garlic and chop your Parmesan so it's fine, and combine.

3. When the grill reaches temperature, place filets on the grill and cook for 4 minutes on each side. After 8 minutes total, spread the filets with the Dijon mustard and dip in the minced garlic and Parmesan cheese mixture and place back on the grill for another 1-2 minutes or until the cheese is melted.

4. Let rest for 5 minutes and serve. Enjoy!

Bbq Brisket Breakfast Tacos

Servings: 6

Cooking Time: 30 Minutes

Ingredients:

- ➢ 4 Pound leftover beef brisket
- ➢ 1/2 Teaspoon extra-virgin olive oil
- ➢ 1 green bell pepper, diced
- ➢ 1 Yellow Bell Pepper, diced
- ➢ 10 eggs
- ➢ 1/2 Cup milk
- ➢ salt and pepper
- ➢ 2 Cup shredded cheddar cheese
- ➢ flour tortillas

Directions:

1. Supply your smoker with wood pellets and follow the start-up procedure. Preheat the grill, with the lid closed, to 375° F.

2. Place leftover brisket in a double layer of foil and warm in grill. Grill: 375 ℉

3. Coat the inside of a cast iron skillet with oil and preheat the skillet in the grill for 10 minutes. When skillet is hot, sauté diced peppers, stirring every few minutes until desired doneness.

4. While peppers are cooking, whisk together the eggs, milk, salt and pepper to taste. Add the beaten eggs to the skillet and scramble. Add cheese to the skillet when the eggs are almost done.

5. Remove eggs and heated brisket from grill. Serve eggs in a tortilla topped with brisket. Top with salsa or guacamole if desired. Enjoy!

Roasted Prime Rib With Mustard And Herbs De Provence

Servings: 8

Cooking Time: 180 Minutes

Ingredients:

- 1 Whole 7-bone prime rib roast
- extra-virgin olive oil
- kosher salt
- coarse ground black pepper
- 2 Cup Dijon mustard
- 2 Cup herbs de Provence

Directions:

1. Note: this recipe requires an overnight marinade, plan ahead. A day before you are ready to cook, prep your prime rib. Trim any excess fat.

2. Coat the prime rib evenly with olive oil to allow the seasoning to adhere. Season all sides of the roast generously with salt and pepper. Next, coat all sides evenly with a layer of Dijon mustard, and season liberally with the herbs de Provence. Let sit in the refrigerator for up to 24 hours, uncovered.

3. Supply your smoker with wood pellets and follow the start-up procedure. Preheat the grill, with the lid closed, to 325° F.

4. Place the prime rib fat side up, directly on the grill grate or on a sheet tray, and roast for 3 to 3 ½ hours, or until the internal temperature reaches 110°F.

5. Pull the prime rib off the grill and allow to rest for one hour. The internal temperature will continue to rise as it rests, you are looking for a finished temp of 130°F for medium rare.

6. Carve the roast. First stand the prime rib upright, and using a sharp, thin-bladed carving knife, carve along the bones, following the curvature of the bones as closely as you can until you cut through the base. Next, slice the roast into even slices, about 1" thick. To carve the bones, stand it upright again and slice along the bones. Enjoy!

Bacon-wrapped Elk Steaks

Servings: 2

Cooking Time: 15 Minutes

Ingredients:

- ➢ 1/4 Cup red wine
- ➢ 2 Tablespoon soy sauce
- ➢ 2 Tablespoon honey
- ➢ 2 Clove garlic, minced
- ➢ 1/4 Teaspoon freshly cracked black pepper
- ➢ 2 Tablespoon rosemary, chopped
- ➢ 1/8 Teaspoon red pepper flakes
- ➢ 2 Pound Elk Steak
- ➢ 1/2 Pound thick-cut bacon

Directions:

1. Make the marinade by whisking together the wine, soy sauce, honey, minced garlic cloves, black pepper, chopped rosemary and red pepper flakes. Slowly drizzle in the olive oil while whisking

2. Add the elk steaks into the marinade and marinate overnight, up to a day or two.

3. Supply your smoker with wood pellets and follow the start-up procedure. Preheat the grill, with the lid closed, to 450° F.

4. Take the steaks out of the marinade; wrap each steak with several pieces of bacon and secure with toothpicks.

5. Place the bacon-wrapped elk steaks directly on the grill grate and cook for 10 to 15 minutes, or until it has reached an internal temperature of 135 degrees F. Rotate halfway through for a good caramelized exterior. Enjoy!

Ancho Pepper Rubbed Brisket

Servings: 12   Cooking Time: 720 Minutes

Ingredients:

- 2 ancho peppers, dried
- 1/2 cup apple cider vinegar
- 9 arbol chilies, dried
- 12 lbs beef brisket, packer cut
- 2 tsp coriander
- 1 tbsp cumin seed, whole
- 2 tsp garlic, granulated
- 1/4 cup kosher salt
- 2 tsp oregano, dried
- 2 tsp smoked paprika
- 3 cups water

Directions:

1. Supply your smoker with wood pellets and follow the start-up procedure. Preheat the grill, with the lid closed, to 350° F. Let it come to temperature. If using a gas or charcoal grill, set it up for medium heat.

2. Place the dried peppers in a large cast iron skillet, then transfer to the grill and cook for 5 minutes, or until fragrant and hot to the touch. Remove from the skillet, and set aside to cool.

3. Add cumin and coriander to the hot skillet, and toast for 1 minute. Remove seeds from the skillet and cool.

4. Remove stems from ancho peppers, then transfer all chilies to a food processor. Pulse a few times to get going, then process on high for 2 minutes, until coarse-ground.

5. Add in garlic, oregano, smoked paprika, and salt. Pulse 10 times to incorporate, then transfer mixture to a bowl.

6. Remove brisket from packaging, set on a cutting board, and blot dry with paper towels.

7. Use a sharp knife to trim the brisket. Start trimming with the fat side down. Trim the silver skin from the flat side, then remove the sides and corners. Remove the fat from around the point. Turn the brisket over and trim any excess fat, leaving around ¼-inch fat thickness.

8. Season the whole brisket with chili pepper rub, then set aside.

9. Fire up your and preheat to Smoke setting. If using a gas or charcoal grill, set it up for low, indirect heat.

10. Place the brisket on the grill, then increase the temperature to 250 F, and smoke until the internal temperature reaches 165°F. After 2 hours, start spraying the brisket every 30 minutes to help retain moisture.

11. Wrap the brisket tightly in butcher paper, then return to the grill and continue to smoke until the internal temperature reaches 200°F.

12. Remove the brisket from the gill and rest for 1 to 2 hours in an insulated cooler before slicing.

Smoked New York Steaks

Servings: 4

Cooking Time: 120 Minutes

Ingredients:

- ➢ 4 (1-inch-thick) New York steaks
- ➢ 2 tablespoons olive oil
- ➢ Salt
- ➢ Freshly ground black pepper

Directions:

1. Supply your smoker with wood pellets and follow the start-up procedure. Preheat the grill, with the lid closed, to 180°F.
2. Rub the steaks all over with olive oil and season both sides with salt and pepper.
3. Place the steaks directly on the grill grate and smoke for 1 hour.
4. Increase the grill's temperature to 375°F and continue to cook until the steaks' internal temperature reaches 145°F for medium-rare.
5. Remove the steaks and let them rest 5 minutes, before slicing and serving.

COCKTAILS RECIPES

Smoked Pumpkin Spice Latte

Servings: 4

Cooking Time: 45 Minutes

Ingredients:

- 1 Small sugar pumpkin
- olive oil
- 1 Can sweetened condensed milk
- 1 Cup whole milk
- 2 Tablespoon Smoked Simple Syrup
- 1 Teaspoon pumpkin pie spice
- pinch of salt
- cinnamon
- whipped cream
- shaved nutmeg
- 8 Ounce smoked cold brew coffee

Directions:

1. Supply your smoker with wood pellets and follow the start-up procedure. Preheat the grill, with the lid closed, to 325° F.

2. Cut the sugar pumpkin in half, scoop out the seeds and discard. Place the pumpkin halves cut side up on a baking sheet and brush lightly with olive oil.

3. Place the sheet tray directly on the grill grate and cook 45 minutes or until the flesh is tender. Remove from heat and place on the counter to cool. Grill: 325 ℉

4. When the pumpkin is cool enough to handle, scoop out the flesh and mash until smooth.

5. Place 3 Tbsp of the pumpkin puree in a separate bowl and reserve the remaining for another use.

6. Add the sweetened condensed milk, whole milk, Traeger Smoked Simple Syrup, pumpkin pie seasoning and salt to the pumpkin puree. Whisk to combine.

7. Pour the cold brew over ice, add desired amount of pumpkin spice creamer and top with whipped cream, cinnamon, and shaved nutmeg if desired. Enjoy!

Grilled Peach Mint Julep

Servings: 2

Cooking Time: 45 Minutes

Ingredients:

- ➢ 2 Whole peach
- ➢ 4 Ounce whiskey
- ➢ 2 Cup sugar
- ➢ 4 Tablespoon pink peppercorns
- ➢ 20 Whole fresh mint leaves, plus more for garnish
- ➢ 2 lime wedge, for garnish
- ➢ 4 Ounce bourbon

Directions:

1. For the Grilled Whiskey Peaches: cut peach into slices, then soak peach slices in whiskey in the refrigerator for 4 to 6 hours.

2. For the Pink Peppercorn Simple Syrup: In a shallow pan, combine sugar, 1 cup water and pink peppercorns.

3. Supply your smoker with wood pellets and follow the start-up procedure. Preheat the grill, with the lid closed, to 180° F.

4. Cook syrup down on the grill for 30 minutes, or until desired smoke flavor has been reached. Remove from the grill. Grill: 180 °F

5. Increase Traeger temperature to 350°F and preheat. Place the whiskey peach slices directly on the grill grate and cook 10 to 12 minutes or until peaches soften and get grill marks. Grill: 350 °F

6. To make the Julep: Muddle 1/2 ounce Pink Peppercorn Simple Syrup with 10 fresh mint leaves and 4 slices of grilled whiskey peaches.

7. Add crushed ice over the rim of the glass. Pour bourbon over the crushed ice and stir. Garnish with 1 large sprig of mint and fresh lime. Enjoy!

Smoked Pineapple Hotel Nacional Cocktail

Servings: 2

Cooking Time: 20 Minutes

Ingredients:

- ➢ 2 pineapple
- ➢ 1/2 Cup water
- ➢ 1/2 Cup sugar
- ➢ 3 Fluid Ounce white rum
- ➢ 1 1/2 Fluid Ounce lime juice
- ➢ 1 1/2 Fluid Ounce Pineapple Syrup
- ➢ 1 Fluid Ounce apricot brandy
- ➢ 2 Dash Angostura bitters

Directions:

1. For the Syrup: Supply your smoker with wood pellets and follow the start-up procedure. Preheat the grill, with the lid closed, to 180° F.

2. Trim both ends of the pineapple, discard the ends. Cut the pineapple into slices about 3/4" thick. Don't worry about the skin, it doesn't hurt to leave it on. Place the pineapple slices on the grill and smoke for about 15 minutes on each sideTrim both ends of the pineapple and discard the ends. Cut the pineapple into slices about 3/4 inch thick. Don't worry about the skin, it doesn't hurt to leave it on. Place the pineapple slices on the grill and smoke for about 15 minutes per side. Grill: 180 °F

3. While the pineapple is smoking, combine 1/4 cup water and sugar in a saucepan over low heat, stirring constantly, until sugar is dissolved. Pour syrup into a large bowl and set aside.

4. When the pineapple is done cooking, cut each slice into eight or so wedges and add the wedges to the bowl with the simple syrup, tossing to coat and cover.

5. Leave the mixture to macerate for at least 4 hours (or up to 24) in the refrigerator, stirring from time to time.

6. Strain the syrup into a clean bowl through a fine-mesh strainer and press on the pineapple with a ladle to extract as much liquid as possible. You can bottle and refrigerate the syrup for up to 4 days.

7. To make the cocktail: Combine the rum, lime juice, pineapple syrup, apricot brandy, and bitters in a cocktail shaker or mixing glass. Fill with ice cubes and shake until cold.

8. Strain into a chilled cocktail glass. Garnish with a lime wheel and serve. Enjoy!

Sunset Margarita

Servings: 2

Cooking Time: 55 Minutes

Ingredients:

- 4 oranges
- 2 Cup plus 1 teaspoon agave
- 1/2 Cup water
- 1 Ounce burnt orange agave
- 3 Ounce reposado tequila
- 1 1/2 Ounce fresh squeezed lime juice
- Jacobsen Salt Co. Cherrywood Smoked Salt

Directions:

1. Supply your smoker with wood pellets and follow the start-up procedure. Preheat the grill, with the lid closed, to 350° F.

2. For the Burnt Orange Agave Syrup: Cut one orange in half and brush cut side with agave. Place cut side down directly on the grill grate and grill for 15 minutes or until grill marks develop. Grill: 350 °F

3. While the orange halves are grilling, slice the other orange and brush both sides of the slices with agave. Place slices directly on the grill grate next to the halves and cook for 15 minutes or until grill marks develop. Grill: 350 °F

4. Remove orange halves from grill grate and let cool. After they have cooled, juice halves and strain. Set aside.

5. Combine 1/4 cup water and agave in a shallow dish and mix well. Remove orange slices from the grill and place in the agave mixture, reserving a few for garnish.

6. Reduce the grill temperature to 180 degrees F and place the shallow dish with agave and oranges directly on the grill grate. Smoke for 40 minutes. Remove from heat and strain. Set aside. Grill: 180 °F

7. To Mix Drink: Rim glass with Jacobsen Smoked Salt. Combine tequila, fresh lime juice, grilled orange juice and burnt orange agave syrup in a glass. Add ice and shake well.

8. Strain into a rimmed glass over clean ice. Garnish with a grilled orange slice. Enjoy!

Smoked Pomegranate Lemonade Cocktail

Servings: 2

Cooking Time: 45 Minutes

Ingredients:

- 32 Ounce POM Juice
- 2 Cup pomegranate seeds
- 3 Ounce vodka
- 8 Ounce lemonade
- lemon wheel, for garnish
- fresh mint, for garnish

Directions:

1. Supply your smoker with wood pellets and follow the start-up procedure. Preheat the grill, with the lid closed, to 225° F.

2. For the Smoked Pomegranate Ice Cubes: Pour one small container of POM juice and 1 cup of pomegranate seeds into a shallow sheet pan. Smoke on the Traeger for 45 minutes. Pull off grill and let sit until cooled. Grill: 180 °F

3. Pour smoked POM juice into ice molds of your choice and put into freezer.

4. When ready to serve, place the frozen pomegranate cubes into a mason jar. Pour vodka and lemonade over the ice cubes.

5. Garnish with a lemon wheel and fresh mint. Enjoy!

Smoke And Bubz Cocktail

Servings: 2

Cooking Time: 45 Minutes

Ingredients:

- ➢ 16 Ounce POM Juice
- ➢ 2 Cup pomegranate seeds
- ➢ 6 Ounce sparkling white wine
- ➢ 2 lemon twist, for garnish
- ➢ 2 Teaspoon pomegranate seeds

Directions:

1. Supply your smoker with wood pellets and follow the start-up procedure. Preheat the grill, with the lid closed, to 180° F.

2. For the Smoked Pomegranate Juice: Pour POM juice and a cup of pomegranate seeds into a shallow sheet pan. Smoke on the Traeger for 45 minutes. Pull off grill, strain, discard seeds and let sit until chilled. Grill: 180 °F

3. Add 1-1/2 ounces of the smoked pomegranate juice to the bottom of a champagne flute.

4. Add sparkling white wine, a few fresh pomegranate seeds and a lemon twist to garnish. Enjoy!

Smoky Scotch & Ginger Cocktail

Servings: 2

Cooking Time: 60 Minutes

Ingredients:

- ➢ 1 Ounce ginger syrup
- ➢ 1/2 Ounce brandied cherry juice
- ➢ 1/2 Ounce agave nectar
- ➢ 4 Ounce scotch
- ➢ 1 1/2 Ounce lemon juice
- ➢ 2 Slices grilled lemon, for garnish
- ➢ 2 cherry, for garnish

Directions:

1. Supply your smoker with wood pellets and follow the start-up procedure. Preheat the grill, with the lid closed, to 180° F.

2. For the smoked ginger cherry syrup: Place ginger syrup, cherry juice and agave nectar in a shallow dish and place the dish directly on the grill grate.

3. Smoke for 60 minutes, or until the mixture has picked up the smoke flavor. Remove from grill and allow to cool for 30 minutes. Grill: 180 °F

4. Place smoked ginger cherry syrup, scotch and lemon juice into a shaker tin and shake with ice. Strain into a glass over fresh ice and garnish with a grilled lemon wheel and cherry. Enjoy!

Smoked Apple Cider

Servings: 2

Cooking Time: 30 Minutes

Ingredients:

- 32 Ounce apple cider
- 2 cinnamon sticks
- 4 whole cloves
- 3 star anise
- 2 Pieces orange peel
- 2 Pieces lemon peel

Directions:

1. Supply your smoker with wood pellets and follow the start-up procedure. Preheat the grill, with the lid closed, to 225° F.

2. Combine the cider, cinnamon stick, star anise, clove, lemon and orange peel in a shallow baking dish.

3. Place directly on the grill grate and smoke for 30 minutes. Remove from grill, strain and transfer to four mugs. Grill: 225 °F

4. Finish with a slice of apple and a cinnamon stick to serve. Enjoy!

Bacon Old-fashioned Cocktail

Servings: 2

Cooking Time: 20 Minutes

Ingredients:

- 16 Slices bacon
- 1/2 Cup warm water (110°F to 115°F)
- 1500 mL bourbon
- 1/2 Fluid Ounce maple syrup
- 4 Dash Angostura bitters
- 2 fresh orange peel

Directions:

1. Smoke bacon prior to making Old Fashioned using this recipe for Applewood Smoked Bacon.

2. To Make Bacon: Supply your smoker with wood pellets and follow the start-up procedure. Preheat the grill, with the lid closed, to 325° F.

3. Place bacon in a single layer on a cooling rack that fits inside a baking sheet pan. Cook in Traeger for 15-20 minutes or until bacon is browned and crispy. Reserve bacon for later. Let the fat cool slightly; you'll use the fat to infuse the bourbon. Grill: 325 °F

4. Combine 1/4 cup of warm (not hot) liquid bacon fat with the entire contents of a 750ml bottle of bourbon in a glass or heavy plastic container.

5. Use a fork to stir well. Let it sit on the counter for a few hours, stirring every so often.

6. After about four hours, put bourbon fat mixture into the freezer. After about an hour, the fat will congeal and you can simply scoop it out with a spoon. You can fine-strain the mixture through a sieve to remove all fat if desired.

7. Combine ingredients with ice and stir until cold. Strain over fresh ice in an Old Fashioned glass and garnish with reserved bacon and orange peel. Enjoy!

Smoked Cold Brew Coffee

Servings: 8

Cooking Time: 120 Minutes

Ingredients:

➢ 12 Ounce coarse ground coffee

➢ heavy cream or milk

➢ sugar

Directions:

1. Place half the coffee grounds in a plastic container and slowly pour 3-1/2 cups water over the top of the grounds. Add remaining grounds and pour another 3-1/2 cups water over the top in a circular motion.

2. Press the grounds down into the water using the back of a spoon. Cover and transfer to the refrigerator and let sit for 18 to 24 hours.

3. Remove from refrigerator and strain into a clean container through a fine mesh strainer or double layer of cheese cloth.

4. Supply your smoker with wood pellets and follow the start-up procedure. Preheat the grill, with the lid closed, to 180° F.

5. Pour cold brew into a shallow baking dish and place directly on the grill grate. Smoke for 1 to 2 hours depending on desired level of smoke. Grill: 180 ˚F

6. Remove from grill and place over an ice bath to cool. Drink as is over ice, with cream or sugar or use in your favorite coffee recipes. Enjoy!

Printed by Libri Plureos GmbH in Hamburg,
Germany